MIKE DROP

DO BUSINESS GOD'S WAY. LIVE LIKE A KING.
CHANGE THE WORLD.

MIKE THAKUR

FIVE
STONES
PRESS

First Edition

Publisher: Five Stones Press, Dallas, Texas

For quantity sales, textbooks, and orders by trade bookstores or wholesalers contact Five Stones Press at publish@fivestonespress.net

Five Stones Press is owned and operated by Five Stones Church, a nonprofit 501c3 religious organization. Press name and logo are trademarked. Contact publisher for use.

Mike Thakur's website is mikethakur.com

Printed in the United States of America

To Troy, Chloe & Zak. I hope this book shapes your futures into the world changers God created you to be.

To Linda, you might not be able to walk on water, or turn it Napa Valley red, but I'm so grateful you're tight with a man that did.

CONTENTS

FOREWORD BY:
BOB GOFF

NEW YORK TIMES BESTSELLING
AUTHOR OF LOVE DOES

My passion is helping people live better lives. It's how I'm wired, and when I connect with other kindred spirits who also love the challenge of creating something amazing for people, I tend to jump in. Mike Thakur and I first met at The Oaks Retreat Center in Southern California. It was during a retreat, but I saw little backing away in Mike's heart for serving God or other people.

I believe it's the same love that inspired him to write **Mike Drop.** Mike and I connected over our common background of walking away from the safe and structured, in exchange for exploring the new and uncharted. Choosing the meaningful paths in life is a challenging yet worthy effort.

His book is a bold call to action for innovators willing to step outside of an antiquated, mission ministry-funding model. Written primarily for current or aspiring entrepreneurs and business owners, **Mike Drop** promises to challenge your approach for effecting tangible Kingdom-focused change. The key to creating that shift is contained in the Bible and has the potential for activating explosive impact to the mission field. I'm not giving away spoilers, but entrepreneurs with a heart to use their business skills to benefit the Kingdom will love Mike's faith-based model, B.O.O.M.

Mike Thakur is the perfect messenger, thanks to his Kingdom purpose over personal profit mindset. His faith-first business approach opens doors for innovation and multiplication that's intentionally focused on responsible stewardship. **Mike Drop** is a fresh look at the old questions of how to combine ministry and the market. If your area of ministry is best suited to the boardroom, **Mike Drop** speaks your language.

Delivering real-world alternatives to simply placing cash in a bucket on Sunday starts with the God-given skills to start businesses and create opportunity. Mike explains how you can start applying those skills for advancing His Kingdom. As Mike points out; If we're ever going to see real change, we're going to have to really change what we're seeing. If you want to create change that benefits the Kingdom, **Mike Drop** is a must read.

Bob Goff,

New York Times Bestselling author of Love Does: Discover a Secretly Incredible Life in an Ordinary World

INTRODUCTION

Have you ever stopped to think about the Great Commission?

I mean really stopped.

You know, the part where Jesus says, "Go and make disciples of all nations, baptizing them in the name of the Father and of the Son and of the Holy Spirit, and teaching them to obey everything I have commanded you."

If you were God and you were developing a plan to save the world, what would it look like? Maybe it's just me, but I think about things like that, and I rarely come to the same conclusion God did. I mean come on, Jesus came to earth for thirty-three years but only went public and ministered to people for three. Seriously? Three years is all we got and that would be enough to save the world?

I think it was a crazy plan.

Why not send Him here in the age of the internet and smartphones?

Or at least have Him invent them back in 30 AD.

Maybe He could have lived for hundreds of years and floated around the world at light speed to carry God's message of hope and love to every person? He is all powerful, right?

It strikes me as fascinating that even in Genesis, at the start of it all, God could have created all kinds of things but instead He chose not to. No cars. No buildings. No planes. No medicine. He didn't even create His own line of designer merch to sell. Doesn't He know anything about marketing?

Even crazier than not making anything we take for granted today (except air, I guess), God didn't seem to be in any kind of hurry either. He was pretty chill about the whole creation and saving the world thing. Time seems to have a different meaning to God than us.

He seemed happy to give us raw materials instead of finished products. Something to work *with*, versus something to work *from*.

He simply created us.

In His image.

The image of a creator.

Someone who takes pleasure and joy in making something from nothing (although technically, we make things from other things unlike Him).

It's important we grasp these early concepts, because there's a formula in Genesis that's been forgotten. It's a formula that tells us how we should live our lives, how we can find our purpose, and how to fulfill His mission.

Before we get to that, I need to know if you're like me.

Do you ever wonder why the world is so crazy?

How, after thousands of years since a miracle-working visit from the Almighty Himself, and after thousands of evangelists (or preachers) have given their lives to spreading the good news, do we still not have it all figured out by now?

Shouldn't the whole world know Jesus loves them already?

Shouldn't we all just love Him back by now, living in some type of utopian bliss?

I'm thinking probably yes.

It's been thousands of years.

And we've seen hundreds of thousands of believers all attempting to do the God thing and share Jesus with the world.

Surely it should be all worked out by now?

But it's not.

If anything, things seem worse than they've ever been.

Whose fault is that?

I don't think it's God's, do you?

That whole "supreme being" and "all-knowing" thing kind of makes sure we can't pin the blame on Him. He wants to save everybody, He loves everybody, and He's made that pretty clear. He's also made it clear that when He wants something to happen, He can make sure it really happens.

If it's not *His* fault, then…

You see where we're going here.

There's no one else to blame really. It's us. We've missed something. We've forgotten something. We've blown it somehow, and because of that, lives may have been lost. Real people may have gone to spend a real eternity in hotel hell, separated from a God who loves them more than I love curry.

Houston, we have a problem.

Maybe you don't think like me, and that's okay. You wouldn't be the first. But as I talk to people in business, life, and in ministry, it seems that there's quite a few that do.

There's a growing chorus of voices who think just maybe we're supposed to have completed the mission by now. We're supposed to have closed the book and be floating around heaven with wings on, seeing how shiny we can make our little section of gold sidewalk as others pass by.

But how do we do that?

What did we get wrong?

And how do we fix it?

This book is a partial answer to questions like these. It's about business, but also more than just business. It's about money, but also more than just money. It's about people, but also more than just people.

This book is about you, me, and the Church, and how we've missed God's best for our lives by passing our calling onto others without realizing it, which is hurting His ability to reach the lost through us.

This book is for entrepreneurs who think their business is too small to make a difference or an impact. It isn't, and I'm going to prove it to you.

This book is for folks who think God works through the professional Church, and bought into idea that we should outsource all ministry to others, when God is sitting in the bleachers waiting for you to step onto the field and start playing the game. The field of marketplace, and entrepreneurship.

This book is for every teenager like young Mike, growing up in a faith that says if you love Jesus and want to serve Him then go to Bible school and professional ministry. There's a better way, and it's my privilege to show it to you here.

Genesis 1 is where it all starts. Beginnings are great because they set the stage. They tell us things that matter. And in Genesis, God told us something really really important.

He told us that He's an entrepreneurial God, who doesn't believe in making things easy. He told us that He's a creative God, who sees things as they could be rather than as they are. He told us that when He wants to give, He likes to do it in a way that includes our input, our effort, and our intelligence. He told us that when He does something, it lasts, and it's not only sustainable, but self-sustaining in nature.

He created a satellite office (earth), put employees on it to manage things (Adam and Eve) and then came down to check in daily, to make sure they were supported.

In other words, He chose work.

Not un-work.

For six days out of seven.

Even though He could have blinked and made everything complete, He didn't. Even though He could have given us the power to create things by simply speaking, He didn't. He made us different.

There's real meaning behind that.

Creation didn't require any extra effort on His part. He didn't need to build in layers, over six consecutive days. He simply chose to. Breaking out the project to model something for us. Sunday through Friday to keep it simple.

It was intentional.

It was purposeful.

It was powerful.

He doesn't do things by accident, and doesn't get things wrong, so every part of the creation story has meaning for us if we dig deep and find it.

Jesus' birth was the same. As the next chapter of God's interaction with His creation opens the New Testament, we see the next clearest example of how God chose to interact directly and personally with His creation.

He came as a baby.

He grew up like you and me.

But then something incredible happens.

At a time when you'd think God would be most interested in saving the world, saving everybody, and helping all of His creation in the most efficient way possible, He does something even crazier than creation.

He sits back and lets Jesus join the family business.

What?

Even crazier is that this was the exact family business God chose to place Jesus. Out of all the people in the whole wide world.

A carpenter.

A creator.

For around fifteen years.

I don't get it.

There's a whole world of people dying, yet God isn't in any kind of hurry. He isn't saving any of them through Jesus that we know of. Hundreds of years of prophecy and hopeful expectation are being fulfilled and this is it?

This is the moment all heaven has been waiting for. Angels cracking open the popcorn as they settle in to binge-watch season two of God's reality TV show.

Apparently, waiting thirty more years for Him to grow was no big deal.

In Genesis, work came first. It did again when Jesus came.

In Genesis, business came first. It did again when Jesus came.

In Genesis, community came second. It did again when Jesus came.

Don't believe me?

Why didn't God make Adam and Eve on day one? Why didn't He create them and include them in the creative process? Why didn't He let them sit on the sidelines and watch, as He painted His canvas with the trees and the sky?

Because this was *His* painting.

His masterpiece.

He was the Creator.

No one was getting in on His action.

The *work* of creation was a good thing. A more important thing than the community that would come out of it.

Why didn't Jesus start helping people when He was twelve? Fifteen? How about twenty? For most of that time He was hustling, working, and being an entrepreneur as He worked at "Joe and Sons" building the family business.

It could have been different.

It could have been anything.

But it wasn't, and by golly do we need to understand why.

There's a pattern we can learn from, a formula we can follow to keep our compass at true north. It will keep our ship from sailing the wrong way and help keep our balance in a world that's lost theirs.

I believe with everything inside of me that if we'd followed this formula, the world would be different.

Saved.

Hanging out with Jesus.

Now.

God uses both the Old and New Testament to show us an optimal, ideal, efficient way for us to partner with Him in taking His message of love to every person He ever created.

That formula is:

Business + Mission = B.O.O.M.

a.k.a. Business Operating On Mission

This whole book is about that concept, and although it's a cool acronym, it's more a statement of the overall intent than a slogan. Conceptually, the idea being that when we fuse our work or business with His mission, we combine two incredible ingredients that ignite to create an explosive impact for His kingdom. On their own, they can be somewhat effective. Together, they deliver *exponentially more* power to the message because God designed a world where the Marketplace of business came first.

If 1+1=2, B.O.O.M. says 1+1=11.

That's why Jesus spent ten to fifteen years working as an entrepreneur, but only three years being Jesus the miracle worker.

That's why Solomon didn't just become the most famous king to ever live, but during his reign, he also became the richest.

That's why God's instruction to Adam and Eve was to go out and be fruitful. To multiply what He'd given them in raw materials. To deliver a return on His initial investment.

Still have doubts?

Did you notice that He didn't create any buildings?

In Exodus, He delivered ten direct commandments for living, yet none of them relate to anything even remotely like what we call Church or ministry today.

Nothing about tithing.

Nothing about praying.

He seemed to be more interested in making sure we weren't eying up our neighbor's wife than He was in telling us to create an institution or movement.

That's because it was never supposed to be about those things. We engage people through life. Through living. Through our daily routines. Through the Marketplace.

Naturally.

Organically.

Genuinely.

I'm not anti-church and I'm not saying we shouldn't have any buildings, but I'm guessing that if we sold a few of them God's kingdom would still be okay. His people could still shower love on the world.

Things are so different today. There are more people. We need ways to gather. There's a different culture to navigate. But what we've made our faith about today isn't what God made our faith about at creation, when He delivered ten hard rules for us to follow, or when Jesus arrived on the scene.

There's something else going on.

Something different.

His original formula for living on earth gives us the answer.

We've moved entrepreneurship, business, and the Marketplace from their original place as the primary vehicles for finding purpose and living in God's image. We've forgotten that these are the vehicles to impact our world and instead, we replaced them with something that was never supposed to be more than a pit stop or a gas station for believers.

To keep our engines running for the road ahead.

God's mandate from the beginning was clear. Our job is to "go and preach the good news." If that doesn't mean that we should all quit our day jobs and become missionaries, then what does it mean?

It means we're supposed to follow His original design and go out, building something amazing, something different, and something impactful, that He can use for His fame and His glory.

To reach others with His love.

It was never supposed to be a ministry, church, or other religious organization carrying out his mission. It was always supposed to be business.

Your business.

The one you're already building (whether leading or supporting the leaders through your work) or the one that's still a dream in your heart and a vision in your mind.

I'm going to show you that business and entrepreneurship were designed by God to propel His kingdom forward in an exponential way.

I'm going to prove to you that the Church and its mission are inadequate and inferior to God's plan without the business-minded leader stepping into his destiny and purpose.

I'm going to show you that you are successful enough today, to take your generosity and resources and do something with them yourself. To stop trusting others with what God has given you.

Finally, I'm going to demonstrate that the fusion of business and mission, led by God's modern-day kings is the only way true kingdom building can happen. That is when real resources can be released into the mission field in a systematic, intentional, and purposeful way while simultaneously ensuring the field is ready to receive them.

As we move through this book it will be helpful if I define a few phrases that are going to come up repeatedly:

1. Church

Church with a big C is the global Church. The institutional Church. Religion. The machine that loves rules, and systems. That has an appetite for things beyond the Great Commission that were never meant to be a part of it. It's the monster we've built and is never satisfied.

2. church

Church with a small c is the local church. The organic church. The grassroots church. The church we read about in the New Testament. Groups of people defined by their community and gathering, not by a building or location. They met in each other's homes. They were lean, mean, impactful machines (metaphorically speaking) who took the gospel around the world as God's community exploded over the first few hundred years. All without buildings.

3. Business owner vs. Entrepreneur

I use these terms interchangeably most of the time. Although an entrepreneur is a business owner, not all business owners are entrepreneurs. Entrepreneurs start 'stuff'. They create out of nothing. They have ideas and take risks. They're the rocket fuel that's lifting the space shuttle. Business owners sometimes don't like risk. They prefer to buy a business after it's profitable, after the painful early years and after everything is figured out.

I believe God has invited both groups into the Marketplace-first lifestyle, but as we go deeper in the pages ahead, there's times I'll break them down to continue highlighting areas for growth.

CHAPTER 1
WHO ARE YOU?

Fairy tales.

Have you ever noticed why we love them so much? It's not the characters, the heroes, or villains. It's not the story, blending high points with low. I think the reason we love them more than anything else is the ending. Because we seem to like happy endings. And why wouldn't we?

We're suckers for happy endings. They close the story out cleanly and leave a sense of satisfaction vs. traumatizing us if something bad were to happen.

Unless it's *Shrek*.

Then I'm not so sure.

This book isn't a fairytale even though it has heroes and villains, highs and lows, and a happy ending to close things out.

Where fairy tales help us is by showing how everyone seems to understand their place. The hero knows he or she is the hero. The sidekick knows they aren't the hero, recognizing they're there to help, but never overshadow.

We struggle because our roles aren't always so clear. We don't always know if we're supposed to be Shrek, or the donkey. We finish our days feeling underwhelmed with our achievements, our productivity, or our results. It's not that we intentionally hate on ourselves, it's that we haven't understood what we're really aiming for on any given day.

Sound familiar or is it just me?

I recently read a book called *Soundtracks* by Jon Acuff, that talks about the 'soundtracks' playing in our minds. I definitely get where he's coming from because I hear soundtracks in my head all the time. They tell me I'm no quarterback on a field of dreams. They tell me I'm not CEO of a hundred-million-dollar business, so I need to do better. They tell me my podcast doesn't reach millions of people around the globe and so the bubble of my existence isn't what it could be.

Some days just feel insignificant.

Some days feel even less than that.

But then I stop and remind myself that I don't get to define success, because someone else already did. He's smarter than me and more powerful too. His name is God, and the only definition of success that matters is His.

I remind myself that I need to build my life and purpose on a foundation that's bigger than my own thoughts, and bigger than culture's definition (which ebbs and flows depending on the hot topics of the time). Defining success needs to be based on a journey and plan God set for our lives.

· · ·

Because the destination of where we're headed actually *is* the journey.

We're not headed anywhere else.

It feels so difficult sometimes to figure out what that journey should look like. Maybe you're different, but I struggle with it a lot. All our journeys are different, so copying someone else's rarely works, and the very leaders we follow often can't relate to the road ahead for entrepreneurs.

As entrepreneurs, we find the answers in Jesus. But not easily. He knows *who* we're called to be and *what* we're called to do. But "being" comes first. Because it's more important. But I wish it was easier to figure this all out. I'm thinking you probably do too.

If I'm called to be a janitor, what's the point in comparing myself to an executive?

If I'm called to be an entrepreneur, what's the point in comparing myself to a preacher?

As believers, we have a Creator and Father who lives in heaven and it's He that sets the standards for our lives. He set them before we were even born, and our only requirement is to:

1. Live up to them.
2. Grow into them.
3. Become the person we were predestined to be.

Many people live their entire lives without ever knowing "WHY?" They exist year after year with no idea of why they're alive or what God's purpose might be for their lives. They repeatedly ask the most basic of questions while they wander around in the dark: "What is the meaning of life?" Have you ever asked that question?

It's important because it shapes everything about who we are and who we'll become. We all want to be happy, but we try to find that happiness in different ways:

…acquiring possessions.
…experiencing pleasure.
…gaining prestige and power.

Real happiness comes from understanding our PURPOSE. The reason we exist isn't to simply exist. There's more to life than that.

God had a purpose for your life when He created you. The biggest hurdle is figuring out what that purpose is and not limiting our perspective as to what it could be. If we don't understand what God says, how can we live the life we were created to live?

We see pastors and understand that God called them to a life of service. But when we look at the world-famous skateboarder Tony Hawk, I'm not so sure we think wow, God created him in his mama's womb to ride skateboards.

Skateboarding. Is that even a thing to God?

I was raised in church and never heard a preacher tell my ten-year-old self that serving God, or His mission, could mean anything other than "full-time ministry" (a.k.a. church work) or heading out to the mission field.

. . .

After thirty-plus years of following Jesus, I can wholeheartedly say they were wrong. If someone had sat me down as a teenager, when I felt the tug and call to serve God, and told me there was another way, a better way to serve God and bring Him fame, I could have saved at least a decade of my life *and* helped more people.

Now, I'm sitting in my rocking chair while smoking a pipe to be the wise old grandad to you, so you don't waste *your* time too. So you don't miss your opportunity because you're chasing the wrong dream while thinking it's the right one. So you don't continue down the road you're on without realizing you were supposed to pull off miles before.

I was trying to answer the call, but the problem was I was picking up someone else's phone. Are you?

Generally, Christians seem to view ministry roles as callings, while everything else is work. Something we do Monday through Friday to fill in the gaps and pay the bills, until we arrive at "me time," when we do what we really want. I've heard preachers say things like "I'm bi-vocational," or "My day job is xxxx." They say it with a tinge of embarrassment, as if they know that we know they're only doing it because their church can't afford to pay them.

I know.

Because I was one of them.

It's the shame that eats you on the inside.

As a church planter who worked two other jobs, that's exactly how I described myself to others. Slightly sheepishly. Always embarrassed. Longing for the day when I could work just one job, God's job, and work it really well.

The problem is that from God's perspective, my "day job" *was* my ministry.

The ministry gig was my side hustle.

I just hadn't realized it yet.

Understanding who God made us to be and accepting that calling over our lives with excitement can be harder than you think. I *knew* beyond any doubt that I was born to preach. I believed 1000 percent that God *called* me to serve Him which could only mean the ministry thing in my mind.

It took me years to recognize that my focus was wrong.

Decades to realize there was a better way.

What can I say, I'm slow.

Gideon

What would you think if someone you never met walked up to you and the first words they said to you were, "Hey, mighty warrior"?

Would you think they're crazy?

A case of mistaken identity?

That's how a young guy called Gideon was greeted. By Jesus. We read about it in the Old Testament, when Jesus showed up and delivered an incredibly specific message to Gideon that blew his socks clean off.[1]

It's not that Gideon looked like the Rock in his movie *Hercules*, or Arnold Schwarzenegger playing Conan.

If he'd looked like them, it would have been less weird.

It *was* weird because he didn't.

Gideon's story of growing up reads more like *Diary of a Wimpy Kid*, which makes me stop reading while asking the question, "What was God doing when He went to visit that crazy day in who knows where?"

*"One day the angel of God came and sat down under the oak in Ophrah that belonged to Joash the Abiezrite, whose son Gideon was threshing wheat in the winepress, out of sight of the Midianites. The angel of God appeared to him and said, '**God is with you, O mighty warrior!**' Gideon replied, 'With me, my master? If God is with us, why has all this happened to us? Where are all the miracle-wonders our parents and grandparents told us about, telling us, "Didn't God deliver us from Egypt?" The fact is, God has nothing to do with us—he has turned us over to Midian.'*
But God faced him directly: 'Go in this strength that is yours. Save Israel from Midian. Haven't I just sent you?'" (Judges 6:11–14).

Being called is great.

But it's only one side of the coin.

The Bible tells us that we're all called so that's not the issue. Interpreting that calling and translating it into something that guides our path is a whole different story.

God appeared to Gideon and called him a mighty warrior.

Except he wasn't a warrior.

There's nothing to suggest he'd even been in a battle before! Who Gideon was created to be in God's eyes was someone Gideon had never seen *in* himself, or believed *of* himself.

If we look at Gideon's response, I think it's the kind of thing we'd say too.

"What you talkin' 'bout, Willis?"

He's a touch more eloquent, but he meant the same thing. He asks for clarification while explaining why God must be wrong. *"My clan is the weakest in Manasseh, and I am the least in my family."*

His understanding of *who* he is, *what* his purpose is, and what he's *called* to do are all based on his rearview mirror.

Looking back, seeing the past and nothing more.

God's view of Gideon is entirely different because God doesn't look back. He only looks forward.

He sees destiny.

He sees a journey.

He sees purpose.

Looking beyond what natural eyes can *see* and looking beyond what history *says*, because God sees the future in exactly the same way as we see the past. It's already happened to Him because He lives outside of time.

There are four things we need to pay attention to in this story:

1. God shows up and calls Gideon a mighty warrior.
2. Gideon complains about all the ways God hasn't helped Israel. *Why has this happened? Where's the miracles we've heard about in the stories?*
3. God ignores everything Gideon said, answering none of his questions and instead, tells Gideon to go save Israel. To step into his purpose. To do what he was made to do.
4. Gideon wasn't a priest, a minister, or any other type of clergy even though there were plenty at the time. He was a regular guy, like you and me, doing a

regular job (in his case, farming) when God
showed up.

I love how God doesn't get drawn into our pity parties,
because right now, today, I'm thinking the exact same thing.

Where's *my* deliverance?

Where's *my* miracle?

Where are you, God, in the drama of Mike's life?

Is it just me, or do you ask these questions too?

His answer to me is the same as His answer to Gideon. He's
answering you with the same thing too.

"Go in this strength that is yours."

The strength was already there, Gideon already had it. It
hadn't been realized. It hadn't been recognized. It hadn't been
unlocked and it hadn't been developed because Gideon was
living a life up to that point based entirely on who *he* saw
himself to be, with no understanding of who God made him
to be. Yet interestingly, something inside of him noticed an
injustice, and felt as though someone should do something
about it.

Could it be that the reason he even noticed the injustice and
wrongs of the people of Israel was because God gave him that
perspective, so he'd go and do something about it?

Wow.

Could it be that the things you and I see that burn our
hearts are in fact the very things *we're* supposed to go out and
fix also? That *they* are our purpose. Our calling. That this is
what we were created for? We'll talk more about these glimpses
later, but for now let's look at the proverbs of Solomon, a wise

guy from Israel who lived years later, after Gideon. He said we should:

"Speak up for those who cannot speak for themselves, for the rights of all who are destitute. Speak up and judge fairly; defend the rights of the poor and needy"
(Proverbs 31:8–9).
The Prophet Isaiah follows up by telling us to:
"Learn to do right; seek justice. Defend the oppressed. Take up the cause of the fatherless; plead the case of the widow"
(Isaiah 1:17).

He repeats this concept later: *"loose the chains of injustice and untie the cords of the yoke… set the oppressed free…share your food with the hungry and provide the poor wanderer with shelter…when you see the naked, clothe them, and don't turn away from family"* (Isaiah 58).

Remember, that's God speaking through him.

Jesus tells us to *"seek first his kingdom and his righteousness"* (Matthew 6:33–34) and to *"Go into all the world and preach the gospel to all creation"* (Mark 16:15) while someone who spent a lot of time with Jesus called Peter wrote that *"Each of you should use whatever gift you have received to serve others, as faithful stewards of God's grace in its various forms"* (1 Peter 4:10–11).

All those verses have something in common.

One thing in common.

They're not limited to specific times or specific people but instead, they're general principles that transcend time. Theologians fret about things like that, because the context of the surrounding verses tells us whether we can take its meaning and apply it to our circumstances and culture today.

On this one we're okay.

We're not mishandling Scripture.

Those words are as relevant and applicable to you and me as they were to the people who heard them first. They are *part* of God's call to all of us throughout the history of time, and they've never changed.

When I've felt like a failure, as if I'd completely missed God's will for my day or my week, I read verses like this and find confidence that if I just start here, I can't be wrong. I can't miss God. Everything will be okay.

There may be more for me to figure out, but if all I do is fulfill these verses, I'm going to be okay when I meet Jesus.

He may even give me a high five.

Along with a bag of cotton candy.

There's something else they have in common. None of them, not one of them, says anything about this being the responsibility of any kind of professional, full-time, paid church staff member or missionary.

Speaking up for others?

I can do that working hundreds of different jobs.

Defending orphans and widows?

Ditto.

Seeking God's kingdom first?

My kids can do that, and they don't even have jobs.

Preaching the gospel?

The monk St. Francis of Assisi was quick to tell us that most of the time, we preach the gospel without even using words even though we can use them too. Our lives were created to be the canvas of God's artistry that the world sees.

These Scriptures aren't talking to professionals, clergy, or ministers doing ministry roles. They're absolutely talking to you and me. Everyday people doing everyday things. The Gideons of our world.

In the first century, the Apostle Paul wrote a letter to a church he started in Corinth. His hope was that: *"all believers continue to live the wonderful lives God has called them to live, according to what he assigns for each person"* (1 Corinthians 7:17).

Again, he wasn't talking to preachers. He was talking to *all* believers.

The church.

You and me.

He was telling us right there, at the beginning of the New Testament church being formed, that God's calling goes far beyond ministry.

It goes to roles.

If you're a nurse, maybe God called you to be one. If you're a teacher, maybe God created you to be one. Imagine if the creator of Facebook went into youth ministry instead, thinking he was supposed to be a student pastor? Billions of people wouldn't be able to connect in the way they can because of his creation.

What would America look like if Vanderbilt decided teaching Sunday school was enough, serving in a small town to be faithful? Railroads sure changed the landscape forever.

In both cases the world would have missed out.

• • •

I believe if you're reading this book that you too could be on the brink of something amazing that the world can't afford to miss out on. It's just that you might not have realized yet what it is. Or worse, you might not have realized that God created you specifically to do that one thing.

What if our calling *is* to live out the entrepreneurial roller coaster so we can impact the world? Sounds a little grand, right? But it's so possible. Impact and change don't always have to be massive, gigantic things. Sometimes it's as simple as making someone's life a little easier. Removing friction and creating margin for them to be a better dad or wife.

We have to stop seeing work as a job, or something outside of and separate from our spiritual lives on Sunday, and start seeing it for what it is, the reason God created us. We need to start teaching our kids that God's call on their life is most likely nothing to do with formal ministry, and everything to do with the gifts and competencies He's put in their lives.

Work *is* the calling.
Sunday the rest.
Refilling the gas tank.
Nothing more.

We rev the engines and race on the other days, every Monday through Saturday, to fulfill God's calling over our lives.

I've heard people say things like, "Oh God's with you, God's called you, you should join the ministry team, the volunteer team, go to Bible college." But I've never heard someone say, "Don't do any of those things, God's calling you to start a business."

Why not?

God is an entrepreneur and we're made in His image.

We still need to operate in the power of the Holy Spirit, but we partner with Him to infuse God's presence into our businesses. How we build them. How we shape our DNA and core values. We intentionally bring God's Word and principles into our entrepreneurial life, not through Bible-bashing everyone around us but by gently, intelligently encompassing the overarching principles of godliness into everything we're doing.

In other words, by building our businesses and living our lives from a biblical foundation and framework that guides, shapes, and molds every thought, decision, and action we take.

I call it living inside the entrepreneurial bubble to support, build, and deliver a business that operates on Mission. B.O.O.M. for short.

We'll get into that later.

For now, we need to accept that we're not living in a world where only a few people are called to serve Jesus. We're *all* called to serve Him which is why the Bible talks about the concept of the "priesthood of *all* believers" in the New Testament. We're *all* priests now, and that means we all carry the priest's responsibility along with God's expectations relating to it.

Understanding that purpose will drive and fuel the mission with every ounce of every resource He's entrusted to us.

Building our lives and businesses on a biblical framework isn't an optional add-on to the Christian faith, like a side of corn bread at the buffet line. It's a requirement if we want to live out our faith in the fullness of God's blessing. He doesn't force it on any of us because He committed to free will a few thousand years ago and hasn't changed His mind yet.

You're the key.

Your understanding of His forgotten formula, the tool by which you unlock the rocket fuel that lifts your efforts into the stratosphere.

---

1. Yes, I did mean Jesus. It's something theologians call a "Christophany," where God came down in human form to hang with us. We can't see God the Father without dying so logic says these instances are Jesus visiting earth.

CHAPTER 2
MATTHEW 25—THE SHEEP AND THE GOATS

I have an amazing bed. I say this to make you jealous because it literally makes me smile every time I get into it.

Seriously.

I talk to it most nights when I get in. I think it likes my kind words and because it looks after me so well, I feel like I owe it a little love!

My pillow's pretty awesome too, along with the super-snug comforter that I wrap myself in. It may just be my happy place, but last night it wasn't.

As I lay down to sleep my thoughts ran wild as I noodled over the day. I realized that because of the choices I've made in life, there are people who've died that didn't know Jesus.

Because of me, it's possible they didn't make it to heaven, but went to the "other" place. You know where. The place we don't like to talk about.

Maybe we think God was kidding, and will break His own rules by letting everyone into heaven anyway, making this whole gospel thing a joke? I don't know. What I do know is that you and I make choices every day that carry eternal ramifications.

It's just that we don't always realize it.

We might not think about it.

But as we go to work, pay our bills, do the church on Sunday thing, and generally look like good, upstanding citizens, everything we do or don't do has an effect on others in this world.

The problem isn't that we deliberately cause others to miss heaven intentionally, it's that we do it unintentionally.

An amazing guy called Keith Green wrote a song about it back in the seventies, based on a story Jesus told:

*"Then the King [Jesus] will turn to those on his right and say, 'You have a special place in my Father's heart. Come and experience the full inheritance of the kingdom realm that has been destined for you from before the foundation of the world! For when you saw me hungry, **you fed me**. When you found me thirsty, **you gave me something to drink**. When I had no place to stay, **you invited me in**, and when I was poorly clothed, **you covered me**. When I was sick, **you tenderly cared for me**, and when I was in prison **you visited me**.'*

Then the godly will answer him, 'Lord, when did we see you hungry or thirsty and give you food and something to drink? When did we see you with no place to stay and invite you in? When did we see you poorly clothed and cover you? When did we see you sick and tenderly care for you, or in prison and visit you?'

And the King will answer them, 'Don't you know? **When you cared**

for one of the least important of these my little ones, my true
brothers and sisters, you demonstrated love for me.'
Then to those on his left the King will say, 'Leave me! For you are
under the curse of eternal fire that has been destined for the devil and
all his demons. For when you saw me hungry, you **refused to give**
me food, *and when you saw me thirsty, you* **refused to give me**
something to drink. *I had no place to stay, and you* **refused to take**
me in as your guest. *When you saw me poorly clothed, you closed*
your hearts and **would not cover me**. *When you saw that I was sick,*
you didn't lift a finger to help me, *and when I was imprisoned,*
you never came to visit me.'
And then those on his left will say, 'Lord, when did we see you
hungry or thirsty and not give you food and something to drink?
When did we see you homeless, or poorly clothed? When did we see
you sick and not help you, or in prison and not visit you?'
Then he will answer them, 'Don't you know? **When you refused to**
help one of the least important among these my little ones, my
true brothers and sisters, you refused to help and honor me.'
And they will depart from his presence and go into eternal punish-
ment. But the godly and beloved 'sheep' will enter into eternal bliss"
(Matthew 25:31–46).

We're not going to dive into deep theology here, but did
you notice Jesus mentioned His kingdom inheritance had been
planned out *before* the foundations of the world were laid?

Anyway, there's a few key concepts we should pay attention to:

1. Both the sheep and the goats were believers.[1] People who would call themselves Christians and profess to living a life of faith.
2. They all thought they were loved by God (they were). Their love wasn't being debated though; it was their actions that were on trial.
3. They all thought they were living their lives in an acceptable way (notice the goats' question: "When did we not help?").
4. They were all surprised to learn that they'd somehow interacted with Jesus in their normal, day-to-day lives.

I may not be Jesus' BFF (John had that place sewn up), but I like to think I know Him a little. Thankfully for us, there was someone who knew Him really, really well.

His kid brother.

James.

Given he grew up around Jesus for thirty years *before* the disciples met Him and knew Jesus when He wasn't *Jesus*, the preacher, healer, and crazy miracle worker, I'm thinking we should pay extra special attention to his thoughts.

James knew Jesus when He was still the carpenter's kid.

Big brother to their motley crew.

Front desk greeter at "Joe & Sons Woodwork."

Errand boy, delivery boy, and doer of everything else that

was needed in the family business as is often the case for the oldest child.

Because James was around Jesus as they grew up, he got to see the "Jesus Christ—Raw" show and understood intricacies about Jesus' nature that we'd never see in three years of public life, a.k.a. the ministry years.

What does this have to do with the sheep and goats story of Matthew? James 2:14–17 tells us:

"What good is it if someone claims to have faith but demonstrates no good works to prove it? How could this kind of faith save anyone? For example, if a brother or sister in the faith is poorly clothed and hungry and you leave them saying, 'Good-bye. I hope you stay warm and have plenty to eat,' but you don't provide them with a coat or even a cup of soup, what good is your faith? So then faith that doesn't involve action is phony."

Sounds pretty similar. No?

James talks about the importance of simple, straightforward actions like buying clothes for someone, giving them food to eat, and taking care of the most basic needs a person could have. Things Jesus talked about in His sheep and goats story.

James closes out this section with the profound statement that if you don't help, your faith is phony, nonsense, or dead.

Awkward.

He's talking to believers.

All believers.

You and me.

That's his audience.

James echoes Jesus' message that those same people wouldn't make it into heaven but would instead, enjoy eternity in hotel hell.

But wait, I know what you're thinking.

The Bible says all we have to do is believe.

Confess with our mouths that Jesus is Lord.

Believe in our hearts that God raised Him from the dead, and everything will be okay.

I hate to break it to you, but if you're pinning everything on that one verse while ignoring the rest you may be in for a surprise.

Remember in Jesus' story *both* groups were seemingly people who thought of themselves in some way at least, as believers. I'm not debating whether their so called faith was real because I have no way of knowing whether they said, or if they said "the prayer" right, when they chose to follow God.

The *only* distinction Jesus is making here, is all about what they *did or didn't* do.

In other words, putting action to our faith might be more important than we may realize.

We get so focused on us, on our world, our comfort, etc. that we forget about the folks we're supposed to help.

The hungry.

The unclothed.

The sick.

What if our lack of help was during their final days of life?

What if they die because we didn't build that water well

someone was talking to us about a few weeks ago? What if they died in hospital and we could have been the last person to visit? What if we'd been the last person who could share with them how much Jesus loved them?

I read a story about a man who carries hundred-dollar bills in his wallet and gives them away to people in need. Whoever he sees, whenever he sees them, he chooses to bless them, and in the process of giving them the hundred-dollar bill, takes the opportunity to explain why he's doing it. He doesn't withhold the cash if they won't listen. He doesn't blackmail them into becoming Christians just for the dough. It's just an easy way to grab someone's attention so he can share about the love that his God has for that person.

I'm not suggesting we stock up on hundred-dollar bills, but I like his style.

We can't disagree with James that our inaction makes us culpable in what happens to others. If the mandate God gave was for us to go out and preach the gospel, then surely we've arrived at a place where doing that doesn't have to involve words. Actions are the key.

James doesn't mention preaching at all.

The only thing he says about mouths and tongues is for us to watch them, and not cuss.

It's our actions that prove how serious our faith is.

Jesus said so too.

From this story, it seems we can make a couple of conclusions. If we get it wrong, we'll see two side effects as our inaction relates to God's kingdom, and they're crucial to how we view our work, our businesses, and the blessings God rains down on us:

1. The goats will lose some type of reward and may not be welcome in God's kingdom when Jesus returns.
2. Other people that the goats failed to help *may* not receive help from anyone else either. As a result, they'll be rejected by God because they never accepted Him to begin with.

Pretty heavy.

If the problem is so clear, then thankfully, so is the solution.

We don't need to live in fear that one day we'll be a goat and not a sheep. We can widen our focus now, and see the harvest fields in the marketplace, recognizing that being generous and helping others is a fundamental part of our gospel mandate. By investing time and energy into learning about the needs of others, developing programs or systems that could help them, and praying for God's guidance and wisdom, you'll be led to an area of focus that God has created for you to impact, in some meaningful way.

He's probably already shown you what that area is. In glimpses throughout your life. We'll talk about how to find them and understand them later.

For some of you, this may sound familiar, but as we move forward here's the rub. The best way to take our calling and giftings and deliver against the goals God set for us (helping orphans and widows, taking care of those less fortunate, etc.)

isn't through an institution or organized religion, but rather through business and entrepreneurship.

In the Marketplace.

One of the best ways we can help is by creating incredible businesses, that in turn create great jobs. We help by creating great cultures that shape our teams, our customers, and our partners as they see us live out this faith-based DNA. We help by living out our faith in the way we interact with those same people, looking to help them grow and realize their God-designed destiny, not just by giving them a paycheck.

Our impact will change how they view purpose and passion.

Our success will deliver even more impact and change by living out God's upside-down kingdom dynamics that say profits were never yours to spend anyway, God's already spent them.

We're just bank tellers handing back to God what was already His, and to illustrate this, I'd like to introduce you to my buddy, Danny.

Danny's a rock star.

He grasped this concept a few years ago.

When he met his wife, Ella.

A few years after getting married, they did what most couples do, starting to plan for a family. Weeks turned into months, but pregnancy seemed to elude them and so after a few visits with their doctors to figure out why, they were hit with discouragement as the doctors explained they had no idea what the problem was.

It turned out that something as natural as having children wasn't going to be as easy for them as it was for others.

Crushed and confused, they did what we all do when we don't understand. They started asking God some big questions.

Why?

Why us?

Why not?

Why? Why? Why?

But then something changed. They began to realize that having children and raising a family can happen in more than one way.

Research pointed to adoption.

Adoption meant months of study, approvals, and prayer.

Finally, the day arrived to bring home their first baby, and they were stoked. But God has a sense of humor so be careful what you pray for! As they were still adjusting, and settling into their new dynamic a few months later, they got a call from the adoption agency. Their baby's birth mother was pregnant again. Given they had baby #1, the adoption agency wanted to see if they'd take baby #2 so the siblings could be raised together.

It seemed logical enough.

So they did.

All was well.

Then the phone rang again.

Now they have three.

In the space of around two and a half years.

And then the phone rang. Again!

Baby #4 was one too many, so they prayed. And one day a neighbor started asking questions about adoption.

Fast-forward to today. Danny and Ella have three boys, and their baby sister lives down the street, adopted by their friends.

Danny and Ella found their calling and mission in those three kids. God didn't need them in Honduras, He needed them in Houston. He didn't need them to volunteer in the kids' ministry, He needed them to minister to three kids specifically.

As they looked around for what Jesus called "the least of these," others in need whom they could help, they chose to make a decision that would change their lives forever. Bringing home three babies. Because of them those kids will grow up loved. Safe. With a future that includes learning about a God who loved them enough He was able to catch the attention of a young married couple, and redirect their focus to where it was needed most.

Because of them, those kids have hope, and by diving in to help, they may just have saved themselves in the process.

Here's the thing though.

All this took money, and I've never come across a church that takes offerings for adoptions. But because of business, because of entrepreneurship, because they had jobs, they were able to take the plunge. Without money coming in, they couldn't have given out, and those babies would be somewhere else.

Most likely not together.

When Danny and Ella had spent all they had, someone else stepped in and paid the rest.

Because their business could afford it.

1. I use the term a little loosely here as there's different schools of thought on this. Some think the goats were believers, others think they were unbelievers and a few more think they fall somewhere in between (folks who think they follow Jesus but don't really live in any way that says they do). Whichever camp you fall in, Jesus does seem to suggest that the goats expected a positive response from him and were surprised when they didn't get it. Based on that, I'm leaning at least to people who think they are believers in some way.

CHAPTER 3
1994

1994 was a big year.

I had my second date with an amazing girl on New Year's Day, got engaged a few months later (when you know, you know), married in the fall and went to Bible college three weeks after the wedding.

I like to move fast.

My new bride and I went to "get us some Jesus" as they say here in the South. I needed Him more than she did, but she came along for the ride.

When it came to perfecting lazy, I'd nailed it up to that point. I'd floated through school with pretty much zero effort and yet, thanks to good genes and quick thinking, still managed to pull out a few good grades. If coasting through school wasn't impressive enough, I'd also held down a high-flying gig at McDonald's as a sixteen-year-old professional burger flipper. No, seriously, I was *amazing* on the grill, and you'll need to listen to my podcast (The Mike Thakur Show) for a full rundown of how amazing we're talking. Season 1, episode 1.

Go listen.

I'll wait.

I still enjoy a McDonald's burger, don't judge me.

1994 was also a big year for someone else, who if I could turn back time I would have interacted with completely differently. His name is Wayne Grudem, and he may be the smartest person I've ever met.

In other words, the complete opposite of 1994 Mike.

I met him in my first year at college, when he stopped by to hang out with the cool kids of theology in the U.K.

Although we had other incredible professors who were also super smart (we're talking Oxford/Cambridge backgrounds which is like Harvard/Stanford for my American readers), only one comes close in my memory to Dr. Wayne Grudem. We'll call him Ted, so I don't embarrass any of the other faculty, and one doctorate degree wasn't enough for him, he had *two*. That might let the cat out of the bag but in my mind, one PhD was enough torture. Two were just plain crazy.

I was never sure if that meant I needed to refer to him as Dr. Dr. (if I did, I figured he'd think I was about to tell a Dr. Dr. joke), Drs. (plural), or something entirely different as a mark of respect to his astounding intelligence, but it turns out my buddy Wayne also had two. I guess that's how you roll in the echelons of theology.

They were like twinsies.

Brothers from another mother.

From different countries and continents.

Both losing a little hair on top. Just saying.

It turned out that Wayne was a theologian and professor from "some" American college (that's how I remember it) who had just released a new book. As a twenty-year-old in a world where the internet was just starting to become real, I didn't know book tours were a thing.

Wayne was a big dog, so touring America wasn't enough. He was touring the world. I'll be touring my mom's street when this comes out.

I don't run in Wayne's circles just yet.

Now when I say he released a book, I'm using the term lightly. I'm calling it a book like we'd say an elephant is a great pet. When you hear the word pet, you're thinking dog or cat. Wayne's book was to books what Clifford was to dogs.

If the book were a bodybuilder, steroids would most definitely have been involved.

He called it *An Introduction to Systematic Theology*. I thought he was a liar, so I need to explain a few things at this point.

1. As I've gotten older, it turns out I'm a bit of a book nerd, but I didn't know I had that gene back then as I'd never read a single book cover to cover so I didn't know what to do with all the emotions and feelings I was experiencing at the time. Even lazy Mike knew *An Introduction to Systematic Theology* was a book he wanted to read. Okay, maybe just parts of it.

2. When he called it *An Introduction*, he'd either been drinking or was being just plain sarcastic. It's thicker than the tires of a Ford Raptor. Seriously. I don't know if my wife can hold it with

one hand. I use mine to work out with and I swear my biceps have grown a couple inches since I started reading it.
I started to wonder if Wayne was really a liar, who'd be turned away by Peter at the pearly gates, but I found out years later that he wasn't. I found an actual systematic theology that didn't have "introduction" in its name.
It was twenty-three volumes.
Each one the size of Wayne's.
I didn't buy that one.

3. Wayne rocks a very similar hairstyle to me, which may or may not have endeared me to him just that little bit more.
Bald is king.
Prove me wrong.

4. I was too innocent to realize that anybody on a worldwide book tour is probably a big deal. Because of this gigantic mistake, I didn't take full advantage of the situation. If you're friends with Bill and Ted, could you see if they'll lend me their time machine so I can go back and do things differently?
I need at least one photo for Instagram.

5. He was smart.
Really, really, really smart.
So smart I realized that pursuing a career as a professor or theologian wasn't going to cut it for me. I didn't like to read back then, and judging by the size of his book, that just wasn't going to work.

I have no idea what he spoke about that day, but I'm pretty sure it was deep.

I do remember it leaving an impression on me and piquing my interest to the point that it fired up the juices of my theological engine which still runs hard today.

At that time though, let's not kid around. It was probably way over my head (I was a first-year student, folks, cut me a little slack here). I walked out of that session the proud new owner of a great doorstop, which, thankfully, I've enjoyed reading over the years and haven't used to hold a door open more than a couple of times.

In the same year, 1994, I was fully committed to the religious, pompous mindset that being "called" by God meant these college years would be like Luke Skywalker's Jedi initiation with Yoda. I was certain that by the time I graduated I'd be turning water into wine, healing the blind, and pulling in crowds of thousands every time I opened my mouth.

It seemed reasonable to me because after all, my voice would be so anointed.

I remembered the scene where Yoda tells Luke that if he only believed, he could raise the X-wing in the swamp, because the force was so strong. I played the scene over and over in my mind, as I was Luke, and the ship was replaced with dead people. They'd be raised back to life through the other force (a.k.a. the Holy Spirit) as the orchestra (angels in my case) built up an audible crescendo in the heavens while I worked.

I'd bought into the lie that serving God could only mean one thing... Formal ministry.

Boy was I wrong.

On both counts.

I still buy my wine at Kroger like everyone else.

Because I was raised Pentecostal, I also buy Band-Aids and Advil too.

So I can "heal" people in need when I meet them.

Jesus stopped a woman bleeding once, I've done it way more times.

If you're not familiar with the unwritten rule of the ministry career jungle, let me break it down for you.

It's kind of like *America's Got Talent* where the rock stars get the golden buzzer, basking in the holy glitter as it shimmers down from above. It has to be Jesus because the glitter's gold, and we all know how much God loves gold.

They head out to become missionaries and change the world, seeing God show up and do the crazy stuff of the New Testament like it's a walk in the park.

If you don't quite achieve golden buzzer status, it's okay. You still get four yeses and progress to the next round. That round is like the NFL draft. You stay home and hope to get picked up by a local church in the first round. But you may still be sitting there in round seven.

If you do get drafted, you'll spend the next decade working your way up the Christian career ladder while earning those McDonald's stars on your employee badge.

Do they even have those anymore? I got all five stars and still have the badge to prove it.

I wear it when I go, to prove I'm worthy of that double quarter pounder with cheese, but I digress.

. . .

Kids' pastor is usually the first job you get, because no one really wants to be one. Most kids are great, but there's always a few little demons to sap the life out of you.

Once the kids have worn you down, you get promoted to youth pastor, because teenagers are so much easier to deal with than five-year-olds. To be fair, handling five-year-olds could be considered a genius training move.

If you clear that hurdle and earn your stripes, then one day, if you're lucky, you might be ready to be an associate pastor and assist the big guns.

When I say assist, it's not like sports where you get a little recognition for it on your stat sheet. Being an associate is more like the assist of a janitor who wipes sweat up off the court. While nobody watches.

It's okay.

One day the heavens will open, the angels will sing, and *the* call will come in. Pastor. Big dog. The man in charge. I imagine it feels like Moses felt when he saw the Red Sea parted but I don't know for sure because I never got the call.

I've seen others who did and in hindsight, I'm kind of glad I didn't. Usually, it meant taking over some failing small church in a hick town no one's ever heard of, and no other pastor really wants. It comes with expectations so low, you wonder how anyone could fail. After all, how hard can it be for you, the newbie pastor, to grow that dwindling church into the next Lakewood?

No one cares that your town only has a population of five thousand people. If you're really anointed, you'll have to grow the whole town, not just your church, to bulk up the pews.

I take full responsibility for any flawed and incorrect theology on this, but in my defense, I wasn't helped by people smarter than me. Nobody in my church, nobody in my college, and nobody in the following years ever sat me down and explained that ministry wasn't the only way to scratch the itch I was feeling.

No one ever even hinted that God was an entrepreneur, loved business, and it's not only okay to be like Him, but that it's a bigger calling than anything else out there.

I spent years chasing my "dream" before realizing that my dream was a nightmare and wasn't God's dream at all.

Maybe I should have listened more at school.

But I wasn't alone.

God was working on Wayne too.

But I didn't know that.

And He didn't tell me. Or if He did, I didn't hear Him.

In 2003 Wayne wrote another book, this time much more realistic for mortals to read. Ninety-three small pages versus 1294 huge pages which converted into small book pages meant it was more like 25,588 pages.

Business for the Glory of God.

I just read it. This week.

God sent that book to me eighteen years ago and here we are today, pondering what might have been. Could this one book have been the catalyst I needed to stop wasting my time chasing Church, and start building a business? I think so.

What took me years to figure out, Wayne figured out faster. That may be connected to him having two doctorate degrees and me having none, but the fact is:

God loves business.

God made business.

Business creates jobs.

Jobs help people.

Making money isn't bad, but loving money is. That last piece I knew.

Phew.

It turns out that creating something *is* imitating God because He's the original creator. Building something *is* imitating God because He's the original builder.

Imitating God is a good thing.

We're supposed to do it, but there's more.

The Bible speaks many times about how important it is for us to help others, to lift up those less fortunate and bring them into God's blessing and purpose for their lives in any way we have the capacity to do. We just talked about it in the last chapter.

Jesus did it through miracles (although He fed a few thousand folks and His team along the way). His kid brother James told us that if we claim to have faith but don't help others then we don't really have faith at all. What we have in that case is something I'll call religiousness. You can pretty much pick out any book of the Bible and somewhere in it is weaved this recurring theme.

The Old Testament law told the harvesters to leave any grain that fell to the ground so when they finished their work for the day, the poor folk could come through and pick the scraps up.

. . .

In today speak, that means if you work at a bank and drop dollar bills on the floor as you're walking by, even one-hundred-dollar bills, just leave them there and don't pick them up so they can help others later.

If you do work at a bank, please don't do this because you might get fired. It was just an illustration. Unless I'm walking right behind you, and then… I'll take care of cleanup on aisle three for you.

The beauty of all this and what we're missing is that the best way, the most perfect way, and frankly the only way to truly imitate God is to do something meaningful, lasting, and self-sustaining. Something that delivers impact and helps the world. Not through missions and ministry alone, but by fusing that mission's heart into entrepreneurship and fueling it through business.

Being generous sounds great, but only if you've got something to be generous with.

It doesn't matter how much money you have; you just can't give it all away to help others because one day there won't be anything left to give, so we need a better solution.

When God spoke to and through Joseph regarding the famine coming to the world, back in Genesis, He didn't say to store up all the food and then give it away.

Not even to Jacob and his family who were God's chosen people.

Joseph sold the food and grain.

When people couldn't pay, he still demanded payment.

God didn't intervene telling Joseph he was doing anything wrong.

Huh.

I'll let Wayne summarize for me because we've already established how smart he is:

"The only long-term solution to world poverty is business because businesses produce goods, and businesses produce jobs. And businesses continue producing goods year after year and continue providing jobs and paying wages year after year."

If only I'd come to that realization as a teenager.

I was so far gone on the notion of ministry being the answer that I missed it. I blew it. Even when the signs of entrepreneurship were clearly there to be seen in my life.

That missed reality would've changed the path of my life in a significant way, and I don't want you to make the same mistake in your lives. I don't want your kids or others around you to make the same mistake either.

It's taken me decades to feel at peace with the idea that business and an entrepreneurial heart aren't just okay with God, but that they're the *primary* purpose for my life, and His *primary* mechanism for advancing society. That *this* is the way God wants us to help people and He gives us the resources to be able to do it.

If that sounds like you, then stop. Think. Maybe it's time to quit too. Maybe chasing the ministry thing isn't really your thing either. Quitting is okay. If you do it looking forward to a better tomorrow, and not because you're lazy. Look at your gifts, your strengths, your capabilities. Maybe they're better suited to the field of Marketplace. Maybe that feeling of unfulfillment is there to nudge you into your destiny. Some of the best advice I ever heard was to simply, "Follow the favor." Where is your favor showing up?

For me, I needed more.

Trusting my mind and my ideas wasn't enough.

I wanted to see just how far the Bible goes in its dialogue around entrepreneurship, around business, and around the concept of God using this mechanism to achieve His goals. The next chapter breaks down even further how God, Jesus, and Paul all confirm for us God's desire that business benefits His people.

CHAPTER 4
BE LIKE GOD

We've already looked at Genesis 1 and the story of creation but if you read it slowly and connect a few dots, it's clearly the story of the first entrepreneurial endeavor. God had heaven, along with multitudes of angels, and one day decided to start something new.

Isn't that the story of so many entrepreneurs?

As He created something out of nothing, He kept fine-tuning His product, polishing the end result until He got it just the way He wanted it.

Entrepreneurship.

He then created Adam and Eve to look after everything, a.k.a. to work in His new satellite location.

Employees in His new business?

Finally, He empowered them (management) and trusted the business of running it to them with occasional checking in for daily progress reports (afternoon walks as the Bible calls it).

Entrepreneurship.

I admit, this is only the start of the biblical narrative but look, there's got to be some weight to the fact it's part of God's very first set of actions.

Before sin happened.

Let's also remember that the Bible tells us we are made in His image. That image wasn't eyes and ears, a nose, and a mouth. It has many levels for sure, but we can't ignore that one of them is this entrepreneurial heart.

The drive and desire to create and to build.

Which is exactly what great entrepreneurs do.

Vanderbilt built railroads that opened up new possibilities for the United States. Rockefeller created oil that could be safely used to transform how people lived. Carnegie created steel that became the bedrock of our modern-day structures. They all operated and functioned in the image of their Creator through the power of entrepreneurship and business.

Did they make a profit?

Absolutely.

Were they perfect examples of godly businessmen?

Absolutely not.

Did they create jobs and pay people wages that enabled those employees to take care of themselves and their families?

Absolutely.

Because that's the best way to live out our faith and provide for others around us.

Most people don't need handouts. They need opportunities, so they can have purpose in their lives.

Take Abraham. Genesis tells us he was successful and wealthy. While it was amassed through God's favor, that favor rested on his entrepreneurial skills, through the buying and selling of livestock. He wasn't a lottery winner. It didn't rain down dollar bills each morning, and they sure didn't grow on a tree.

Solomon was the richest king that ever lived, and a quick dive into the text reveals he was a razor-sharp businessman. He had trading ships that went out and…traded. Precious items and cargo, year after year after year. He wasn't wealthy because of the taxes coming in. There wasn't enough money in Israel to make him unimaginably rich. He was wealthy because of his entrepreneurial heart and God's blessing on it. That wealth propelled him forward as king to be able to fund and finance God's purposes for a nation.

If you didn't already know, Solomon was richer than Bezos, Musk, Gates, and Buffet all put together. Estimates put Solomon's wealth in the trillions of dollars.

That's trillions, with a capital *T*.

If this had been possible some other way, wouldn't that have been easier? Couldn't God have simply rained down gold like the manna we read about in the story of Moses?

Couldn't they have stumbled across a gold mine and simply dug it up rather than working for it?

It's reasonable to conclude that this was the only way because it *is* the way God chose to work in Solomon's life.

Work is good.

Entrepreneurship is good.

Creating and building things are actions that allow us to be like Daddy God.

· · ·

But are there other examples we can look to and learn from in the Bible?

Jesus

Jesus had a few things to say about God's kingdom and expectations.

"Heaven's kingdom is like a wealthy man who went on a long journey and summoned all his trusted servants and assigned his financial management over to them. Before he left on his journey, he entrusted a bag of five thousand gold coins to one of his servants, to another a bag of two thousand gold coins, and to the third a bag of one thousand gold coins, each according to his ability to manage.

The one entrusted with five thousand gold coins immediately went out and traded with the money, and he doubled his investment. In the same way, the one who was entrusted with two thousand gold coins traded with the sum and likewise doubled his investment. But the one who had been entrusted with one thousand gold coins dug a hole in the ground and buried his master's money.

After much time had passed, the master returned to settle accounts with his servants. The one who was entrusted with five thousand gold coins came and brought ten thousand, saying, 'See, I have doubled your money.'

Commending his servant, the master replied, 'You have done well, and proven yourself to be my loyal and trustworthy servant. Because you have been a faithful steward to manage a small sum, now I will put you in charge of much, much more. You will experience the delight of your master, who will say to you, "Enter into the joy of your Lord!"'

Then the one who had been entrusted with two thousand gold coins came in and said, 'See, my master, I have doubled what you have entrusted to me.'

Commending his servant, the master replied, 'You have done well, and proven yourself to be my loyal and trustworthy servant. Because you were faithful to manage a small sum, now I will put you in charge of much, much more. You will experience the delight of your master, who will say to you, "Enter into the joy of your Lord!"'

Then the one who had been entrusted with one thousand gold coins came to his master and said, 'Look, sir. I know that you are a hard man to please and you're a shrewd and ruthless businessman who grows rich on the backs of others. I was afraid of you, so I went and hid your money and buried it in the ground. But here it is—take it, it's yours.'

But his master said to him, 'You're an untrustworthy and lazy servant! If you knew I was a shrewd and ruthless businessman who always makes a profit, why didn't you deposit my money in the bank? Then I would have received it all back with interest when I returned. But because you were unfaithful, I will take the one thousand gold coins and give them to the one who has ten thousand. For the one who has will be given more, until he overflows with abundance. And the one with hardly anything, even what little he has will be taken from him' (Matthew 25:14–29).

Let's pull a few key things from this passage to help us understand God's view of business and kingdom from the perspective of His Son.

1. This parable is ultimately about Jesus.
Theologians agree that Jesus uses this story to explain that He

gives us something valuable (giftings, the gospel message, resources, and finances, etc.) and will return one day expecting that we used them well, growing them into something more that benefits a kingdom return.

Like a business owner.

2. Jesus uses language that His audience would understand and that was intentional. It was that of a landowner or business owner entrusting his employees. There are other examples He could have used but He chose to go this route for a reason.

3. The landowner returned and was pleased with both of his staff who doubled their money. The amount was irrelevant, the fact that they grew it was all that mattered.

4. The return was double. Not fivefold or tenfold. His expectations were reasonable.

5. He was unhappy with the employee who didn't show a return even though he hadn't lost anything either.

The expectation wasn't for the status quo to remain.

6. Risk was expected. They traded. But it was a calculated, educated, intentional risk.

7. The successful employees were rewarded with more. They'd proven themselves trustworthy so why wouldn't they be?

8. The unsuccessful employee wasn't just terminated, but his share was given to the most trustworthy employee. The one who'd been given the most responsibility to begin with and proven what a smart move that was.

All these thoughts are in complete harmony with our modern-day understanding of business and entrepreneurship. Investing capital, hiring employees, trusting them, delegating responsibility, holding them accountable, expecting growth, and rewarding success. There's no doubt that this parable, from Jesus' lips, clearly supports the idea of business. If Jesus was happy to use business as an example to teach from, then by inference alone that has to mean on some level, that He is *for* business and not against it.

But supporting the idea still isn't enough. I wanted to see if Scripture actively suggests business as *the* ideal way to fund, support, and deliver missions to the world. To see if it was God's best solution to reaching people.

As it happens, not only does Scripture say it.

It screams it.

Paul

Paul is the apostle who single-handedly wrote most of the New Testament. He's responsible for more of the growth in the early church than any other individual recorded.

More than any of the twelve disciples who ran around with Jesus for three years.

You might even call him the father of the non-Jewish church as he spent his time evangelizing outside of Israel, leaving the Jews to Peter and the other apostles.

We see multiple mentions of Paul's day job as a tentmaker in the New Testament, but the book of Acts (chapter 18) is the most helpful.

Not because of what it says, but because of who wrote it and why.

Dr. Luke wrote the books of Luke and Acts as a single piece of work for someone named Theophilus. We aren't entirely sure who Theophilus was, but we do know that Luke was trying to communicate all the things that had happened in a single, comprehensive document, for someone who was likely well educated, and eager to learn about this Christianity thing that was causing a ruckus.

Luke's viewpoint, or angle if you like, is that Christian service and ministry, what we call the Christian walk, is really about Spirit-filled believers living their everyday lives as witnesses. Not going out and "witnessing" from time to time as an activity but living out our faith as a witness *all* the time through our normal, everyday activities.

Did you catch that?

It's not something we *do*, it's something we *are*.

It's from this baseline thought and within this context that we need to consider what he wrote. If he's suggesting that our lives are witnesses to the power of the gospel (which he is), then every part of our lives, including our work, is a part of that mission. Work isn't something we do in isolation, to fund the rest of our lives so that we can then go and do whatever it is that we really want. Plenty of people live that way, longing for the weekend when they can be the real them, but that isn't God's best for anyone.

We're all called to minister.

Like Jesus.

Whether it's getting water from the store (our version of a well) or sleeping on a boat and being rudely awoken by friends panicking about a little rain and wind.

Applied to Paul, we have to question why the smartest, most educated, and most powerful apostle was "wasting" his time making tents.

Shouldn't he have been preaching more?

Shouldn't he have been writing more?

Wasn't his time more valuable than tent making?

I'd have said yes.

But apparently not.

We're thinking about it all wrong.

He didn't make tents because he needed to support himself financially. He had the support but didn't want to use it. He wanted to preserve the resources. Partly because the mission needed it more, and partly because he realized tent making was part of his ministry.

By making tents he could engage with customers and suppliers, groups of people he could shine God's love to and dive into deep conversation with.

By making tents he could place himself in the middle of the marketplace, the physical marketplace, every single day.

By making tents he could create profit (whether it was a large or small one doesn't matter) that would sustain not just him, but the mission, as well as the others working alongside him.[1] This is funny because I have a friend called John, who's a custom home builder in Dallas (today's version of a tentmaker). God told him to start building homes years ago and John has used it as a way to reach countless people with the gospel through their biblical approach and methodology toward people and business. He's literally living today like Paul did then, which I think is pretty cool, and he's seeing people's lives touched over and over again along the way.

. . .

When Paul made tents, he was imitating his Creator, and honoring the words of Jesus he so clearly knew and remembered:

*"I haven't been after your money or any of your possessions. You all know that I've worked with my hands to meet my own needs and the needs of those who've served with me. **I've left you an example of how you should serve and take care of those who are weak.** For we must always cherish the words of our Lord Jesus, who taught, 'Giving brings a far greater blessing than receiving'"* (Acts 20:33–35).

Because of Paul's willingness to break the mold, others were able to minister alongside him (and logically, probably made tents with him so we might even call them employees).

The most powerful verse (in bold) is where we see Paul telling us his why.

Why did he choose this route, which was opposite of how every other apostle did things?

He articulates that he chose this path (choosing to do less "ministry" in the traditional sense like preaching), so he could be an *example* to us. An example that shows us how *we* are to operate because the only reason examples exist is so we can learn from them.

Paul expected us to imitate him as he imitated God.

He didn't do it because he had to.

He didn't do it because he wanted to.

He did it because he needed to.

. . .

He needed to demonstrate for us a correct theology of work and entrepreneurship in relation to mission and kingdom dynamics.

We're supposed to follow his example because it fuels the mission better, makes funds go further, and opens up a whole new world of opportunity. We're supposed to follow his example because it helps spread the gospel by placing us and God's work in us on full display in the marketplace, where nonbelievers are.

This is the true ministry of taking the gospel outside the Church walls and shining a light on its work in each one of us.

It's a powerful statement that Paul, the first apostle who didn't live out of the money bag Judas kept on behalf of Jesus to fund ministry, decided against asking for or receiving any financial support. I'm not saying he didn't stay at someone's house and let them take care of him. But I am saying it doesn't seem as though he was sending out a collection plate every time he spoke.

He took it upon himself to evolve the thinking of the day into a better way of how ministry should perform, and how mission should be funded.

Through entrepreneurship.

Finally, let's not forget Jesus the son of Joseph, carpenter of Nazareth. Of all the families He could have been born into, you'd think given the overwhelming example of the Old Testament that He would have been born a shepherd.

They were all shepherds.

Jacob, David, you name it.

But Jesus wasn't.

He was born into business.

Entrepreneurship.

Carpentry.

He made stuff.

Have you ever thought about what He did from being a teenager through the age of thirty when His ministry began? You realize He spent more of His earthly life in business than ministry, right?

Dealing with customers, suppliers, quality control issues (maybe), and everything else we entrepreneurs deal with. He did it for years and I think Paul was absolutely aware of this when God gave him the tent making idea.

Some folks think Jesus' entire ministry could have been funded from and supported by His earlier work as a carpenter, or at the very least the family business. We never read of Jesus or the disciples taking up an offering or asking anyone to tithe, yet they seemed to have a kitty of petty cash when they needed it. And when they didn't, He had them go fish.

God opened up the Bible as a creator, an entrepreneur building His kingdom.

Solomon created wealth not only for himself, but his entire kingdom through the power of business.

Jesus grew up working in the family business.

Paul took cues from all these things and saw a better way than simply asking for free money. He saw the power of entrepreneurship as the ideal vehicle to transport the gospel across the known world *because* of business, and as a bonus, funded by it.

.   .   .

Now that we've established the absolute connection between business, entrepreneurship, and mission, it's time to understand the different roles each of us play in how this works today. Solomon was a king, but the Bible was filled with priests and prophets too.

---

1. Some historians don't think Paul could have built any kind of meaningful business in each city given the time it takes to establish roots which would have been tough for someone on the road as much as he was. That said, the text does seem as though he was able to do some work that created revenue.

CHAPTER 5
KINGS

If you've ever wondered what's wrong with Christianity, I'm here to tell you you're not alone. I've wondered about it too.

For years.

If God is so smart, so amazing, and so powerful, and if the Church has been firing on all cylinders for a couple thousand years, then what on earth happened for us to be where we are today?

We've got church buildings next to other church buildings who never speak and just do their own thing. We've got Christians who lie, cheat, steal, and kill just like everyone else.

But on Sundays they sing about Jesus.

We've got a world where billions of people don't have regular access to clean water while we're sprinkling our lawns twice a day all summer long.

It can't be God, so it has to be us.

We've missed something.

We've got something wrong.

Let's figure out what it is so we can fix it. To do that, we need to understand a few of the major Old Testament roles, because although God interacted with Adam directly in the beginning, once he sinned and messed it all up, plan B came into effect.

Prophet

The Old Testament prophets are some of my favorite characters. They're identified easily because they're the ones hearing words directly from God and communicating those words to people. God didn't speak directly to everyone back then, choosing to speak through specific people, oftentimes in crazy ways, instead.

Isaiah ran around naked for a few months while telling everyone God told Him to do it. If he ran past me saying that, I'd think Isaiah was crazy.

Moses told Pharaoh a whole bunch of plagues was on the way to decimate his land. He didn't believe him. Turns out that wasn't so smart.

Prophets also performed the occasional miracle to spice things up. Want to stop rain for a few years? No problem. Elijah prayed a prayer like no other prayer and no rain fell for years, until he prayed it would rain again, and then it did.

Need to bring someone back to life? Elisha's got you covered. Raising a young boy back to life for his mom, just like Jesus raised a little girl years later.

. . .

There are so many miraculous events in the Old Testament it's amazing, and almost all of them are tied to an individual prophet of the day.

The key here is that prophets were chosen and ordained by God to serve in a specific way, but they're also famous for what they didn't do. Some things were someone else's gig.

Priest

The priest was different. They represented us to God. We might say their communication was upward (from us to God) whereas the prophet's communication was downward (from God to us).

Priests served in the temple, offering sacrifices on behalf of the people, and interceding for their sin. They also had to be born into the family. If you weren't, you were out of luck. They descended from the line of Moses' little brother, Aaron, and the tribe of Levi, hence the nickname "Levitical priests."

The priests were also unique because they weren't allowed to work in the way everyone else did. Their role was priest, not farmer, shepherd, or carpenter. As a result, God introduced a tax system called tithing that would go to funding the priests, taking care of them and their families.

King

God's plan was never for Israel to have an earthly king because He was King and He wanted to lead them. He got upset when they asked for a king so they could be like all the other countries around them, because He doesn't like copycats. He's an original and was building an original nation under a different mold.

But God being God, He respected their free will and gave them a king too, modifying His plans to work with His creation.

The king served as God's appointed agent to rule, and they were expected to rule well, knowing God's laws (which meant spending time learning them). They also had to make sure justice was seen throughout the kingdom. For everyone. As a bonus, they were often military leaders who would lead the armies and defend Israel, even engaging in offensive warfare when necessary.

You see these qualities in the lives of David and Solomon, the second and third kings of Israel. I get the feeling David was more Maximus from *Gladiator* rather than Schwarzenegger from *Terminator*. His biceps might not have been huge, but his heart was, and it captured God's attention.

Solomon was his son, but his fame wasn't through battle, it was through brains. His ruling was so legendary that royalty from other countries came just to see him in action. They couldn't believe the stories they'd heard without seeing them for themselves.

With his wisdom came justice and wealth.

Serious wealth.

Although it didn't happen often, when the three roles functioned together in harmony, Old Testament life was pretty perfect for God's people.

· · ·

David and Nathan

King David woke one morning with an idea. He called for the prophet on duty and Nathan arrived, listening to king David tell him it was time to build a home for God. David felt guilty because he'd built himself a spectacular palace, but all the God stuff still happened in tents. He thought God should have something impressive to call home too, but he didn't want to do anything without checking God was cool with it. David's heart and motives were in the right place, and there's five key concepts here that tie in business and wealth to their relationship with mission and kingdom in this story.

1. The king had the idea. Not the prophet, or the priest.

This idea was big. It needed resources to make it happen and it came from the king, the leader who had control of the resources needed to make it happen.

2. The king needed the prophet to ask God if He approved, and to rubber-stamp the idea.

Just because David had an idea, he knew better than to only rely on his own intellect. He sought out someone else who he knew heard from God to check and validate.[1]

3. The prophet (and subsequently priest) bought into the idea once they knew God approved.

They didn't get upset because they hadn't had the idea. They supported the king in *his* idea, recognizing how it would benefit them and the people.

4. The king committed to funding the idea.

David put his money where his mouth was. Billions. He committed his time and intelligence to planning, as well as significant resources to pay for it so that the idea could become a reality. Centuries later, Jesus would walk through its halls and teach from its steps.

5. They each stayed within their respective roles.

There's little overlap between who does what and who doesn't. They had a healthy and mutual respect for one another, understanding that they were all ultimately appointed and anointed by God.

There's another Old Testament king who wasn't a believer and didn't follow Jewish traditions. A man named Nehemiah happened to have pretty good access to this King because he was his cupbearer.[2]

Nehemiah wasn't a priest or prophet, just a regular guy, like you and me, who happened to work for someone wealthy and powerful. He heard stories about his hometown (Jerusalem) being devastated from war, and asked God to do something. God held a mirror back at him and said, "Okay then, go do something…"

*"The king said to me, '**What is it you want?**'*
*Then I prayed to the God of heaven, and I answered the king, 'If it pleases the king and if your servant has found favor in his sight, let him send me to the city in Judah where my ancestors are buried **so that I can rebuild it.**'*
Then the king, with the queen sitting beside him, asked me, 'How long will your journey take, and when will you get back?' It pleased the king to send me; so, I set a time.
*I also said to him, 'If it pleases the king, **may I have letters** to the governors of Trans-Euphrates, so that they will provide me safe-conduct until I arrive in Judah? And **may I have a letter** to Asaph,*

*keeper of the royal park, so he will **give me timber** to make beams for the gates of the citadel by the temple and for the city wall and for the residence I will occupy?' And because the gracious hand of my God was on me, the king granted my requests"* (Nehemiah 2:4–8).

It makes me think of Joseph when I read this, because like Nehemiah, he also seized an opportunity that required massive resources. Resources that weren't his. They both needed the resources of their "bosses," the kings, to accomplish what they needed to.

Who paid to rebuild Jerusalem?

Nehemiah?

Nope.

The people after he convinced them God was behind this new building campaign?

Nope again.

The king did.

The guy with the money, influence, and power that could make it happen. The fact he didn't believe in God *didn't matter.* God accomplished what He needed to. Maybe that's what the Bible means when God says in Psalm 50 that, *"the entire world and everything it contains is mine."*

In all three stories (David, Joseph, and Nehemiah), we see God achieve an end result that is significant, through a journey that costs a huge amount, that is funded by the leader, ruler, or king of the day. The one who controls the resources.

At no point does God nudge the spiritual leaders to step up and do anything.

Anything.

He doesn't ask them to start a fundraising campaign.

He doesn't ask them to start a prayer and fasting campaign.

He doesn't follow a step-by-step pattern but works through and speaks through non-ministry people to bring ideas to mind and then funds them through the folks who have the ability to simply make it happen.

Today, that would be entrepreneurs. Business leaders. The powerbrokers of today. Why spend the time and energy rallying people around an idea who can't bring it to life, when one specific person can?

Even if Nehemiah had the money, he still needed protection, so King Artaxerxes was the only person who could single-handedly do everything Nehemiah (and God) needed.

When Jesus came, He functioned in a way that united the three roles, hearing directly from God, interceding on our behalf while standing in the gap between us and God, and leading / administering justice like an Old Testament king.

He didn't just fulfill the roles but took them all the way up to eleven on the volume dial.

He didn't just make sacrifices for our sin; He became the perfect sacrifice for it.

He didn't just become one in a long line of many kings; He became the King above every other king.

He didn't just hear from God on an occasional basis; He communicated with God in a way no-one had ever communicated before.

The Priesthood of All Believers

This all matters because Jesus was setting out a pattern that our faith would be built on. Peter explained it while throwing down some dynamite in his first letter to the church. He described the results of Jesus' work on the cross as well as its impact on us, as believers. Because Jesus fulfilled the three key roles that God had worked through up to that point, we needed to understand the new plan.

*"Come and be his 'living stones' who are continually being assembled into a sanctuary for God. For now **you serve as holy priests**, offering up spiritual sacrifices that he readily accepts through Jesus Christ...*
*They keep stumbling over the message because they refuse to believe it. And this they were destined to do. But you are God's chosen treasure—**priests** who are **kings**, a spiritual 'nation' set apart as God's devoted ones. He called you out of darkness to experience his marvelous light, and now he claims you as his very own. He did this so that you would broadcast his glorious wonders throughout the world"* (1 Peter 2:4–9).

Peter is telling us that we don't need to look for a priest or prophet now, because thanks to Jesus, we are one. We don't need a king now because thanks to Jesus, we can be kings too (with a small *k*). We're not replacing Jesus as *the* King, but as entrepreneurs and business leaders, we can function in a kingly role as we lead people and control resources that can impact the world for Jesus.

As New Testament believers, we inherit the functions or roles that come with those Old Testament titles because our faith is personal, directly connected to God instead of working through third parties.

As believers today, we can help bring others to God and God to others (priests).

As believers, we can speak on behalf of the most vulnerable among us (prophets).

As believers, we can use our time, money, and resources for the benefit of others (kings).

Even though we can function in the three roles, some folks seem to function in certain ones a whole lot better than others.

The Old Testament kings were anointed, called, and gifted to acquire resources. As a result, they accumulated and acquired wealth. They traded and did business for wealth. They plundered in war for wealth. And they stored it up, readily using it when needed. Sometimes this was directed by God while at other times it was accomplished by God through someone else's ideas, without them even realizing.

What does that sound like?

Who are the kings of today?

Who is ruling their kingdom ready for God to show up and ask them for help?

You guessed it. Entrepreneurs.

Entrepreneurs are today's version of those old-time kings. We're the modern-day bankers as far as God is concerned. We rule over our worlds of influence, operating within boundaries we created and built, while acquiring and growing wealth, influence, and power.

We have a specific anointing to do this, but the Bible is pretty clear that God's blessings over our businesses aren't there so we can buy more stuff.

Remember Psalm 50?

We bring a level of expertise, intelligence, and experience to the kingdom and God's mission that might not be there otherwise. We bring a level of impact and insight that would otherwise be missed and most importantly, we bring our piggy banks with us because we're the ones holding the keys.

A quick glance over the wealthiest people in the world reveals they all amassed their fortunes through business. Here's the top five.

1. Jeff Bezos—Founder of Amazon.
2. Elon Musk—Founder of Tesla.
3. Bernard Arnault—LVMH (the world's largest luxury goods business).
4. Bill Gates—Founder of Microsoft.
5. Mark Zuckerberg—Founder of Facebook

Clearly, I'm not suggesting they're all godly guys, as their actions and comments suggest for the most part that they're not. However, the principle of business and its ability to create wealth hasn't changed. It's an indisputable fact.

It's just a little hollow without the injection of God's spirit to bring the sizzle.

There is no other way fortunes are acquired, and as we saw with Solomon, God fulfilled His promise of riches by using

Solomon's intelligence and skill from a business (trading) perspective to grow the wealth.

Today, Christianity and the Church are anemic in their quest to fulfill the Great Commission because we've redefined the expectations of believers into something they should never have been. We've made pastors professionals, expecting them to hear from God, work for God, *and* figure out how to pay for it all by themselves.

Sure, they see some successes, but compared to what could be achieved, it's a glimpse, a firstfruits at best.

Why?

For one, the New Testament church didn't even have professional pastors. Sure, it had people who were pastoral, but that's a descriptive word, not a job title.

We should have recognized long ago, as they did in the early centuries, that the concept of a priesthood of all believers means everything changed. It meant *every believer* would now be a priest, a prophet, and king. We all have a part to play in mission and can't simply continue with the spectator sport of twenty-first-century American Christianity.

We play our part in this mission through our day-to-day businesses, not by volunteering as an usher on Sunday mornings.

We play our part by recognizing that our call to entrepreneurship is a call to mission, it's just wrapped around business rather than begging.

Until that realization sits deep in our hearts the Church will remain handicapped.

· · ·

The same goes for pastors who've bought into the lie that they are the professionals, and all ministry funnels through the Church, while everyone in the pews should just get behind their ideas and fund them.

No.

That's wrong.

It's not what Jesus intended at all.

People won't get behind them and people don't get behind them. Today's kings absolutely won't, because many of them are smarter, more capable, and better suited to execute on kingdom projects than the people supposedly leading them.

Kings ask different questions.

Kings need different answers.

We expect measurables and metrics, we expect systems and processes. We won't accept blind trust; Jimmy Swaggart put an end to unintelligent giving with his gold-plated toilets.

If you're thinking your pastor is different, that he's entrepreneurial and gifted in business so your church has it right, it doesn't, and he probably doesn't either. If he's called and gifted in entrepreneurship, it's probably because he's supposed to be one. Out there. On the field of marketplace, and his impact will be limited until he or she steps up into that realization.

My business was built and has been used as a catalyst for mission since inception.

Period.

There was no other agenda.

That was the plan all along. It's been a multiyear project to understand and formulate the things I'm now sharing here.

Rather than be a town crier, I wanted to put my money where my mouth is and live out this message.

We didn't need the money. As chief operating officer of a global security firm known as the "Secret Service for billionaires" life was pretty good.

But now, in this experimental business, as we've grown our revenues, we've grown our profit, and as we've grown our profit, we've grown our ability to help others. To invest for kingdom impact.

Why?

Because I don't think Jesus was kidding when He said He expects a return.

Do you?

Recently, we spent time talking to a ministry run by great people, doing great work, and completely in line with one of the core focus areas of our nonprofit organization to support. After some smaller tests, on specific items and projects, we started dreaming bigger with them, looking for ways to deliver significant impact together. It was so exciting.

After a few conversations and a little back and forth we had a few questions, because it's important we understand how God's money will deliver on that return He's looking for.

After the questions, came crickets. Silence.

Nothing.

No more emails.

Communication stopped.

It seemed that either the project wasn't something they were interested in pursuing further, or if they were, then not with us. Given we were talking about an evangelism-based idea, I figured it wasn't the project that was the problem.

I share the story because I heard a few months later that their annual gala raised only around half of the money they set as the goal. Now, they were reaching out to friends and donors asking for more, because they were in a hole.

Had they understood the principles we've uncovered in this chapter, they'd have realized that aligning with a modern-day king (entrepreneur) would have brought a different dynamic to their ministry, easing the stresses associated with fundraising and donor management.

Instead of feeling under pressure, they could have been feeling freedom.

Instead of feeling alone, they could have been feeling supported, because kings don't come empty handed. They bring their team along for the ride with their strengths, smarts, and sass!

Instead of continuing the cycle of begging, they could have been watching, learning, and growing from their exposure to the kingly mindset, until they reached the point where they were ready to build a self-sustaining revenue stream for their work, just like Paul.

How can I be so sure?

Because we were happy to step up.

We were going to support and help not just as a nonprofit organization, but through my for-profit business also. My team loves to be a part of the things we work on beyond our core business so why wouldn't we? It's what we hire for!

· · ·

We were going to write a check that was almost the same amount as the entire goal of their fundraising gala. Instead of being short by 50 percent, they'd have been over budget.

But we didn't.

Because they blew it.

Let's talk about why in the next chapter.

---

1. As a side note, this is a great practice to have even today. As we seek God's guidance and approval for the decisions we make in our lives, having trustworthy friends who are also prayerful and hear from God can be a great way to make sure we aren't making a mistake in some way, even with the best intentions.
2. You can go hear a great message on this story that came out mid-April 2021 by my buddy Daniel Fusco on YouTube.

CHAPTER 6
THINK DIFFERENT

In 1390, a man by the name of John Gower wrote a Middle English text called "Confessio Amantis," in which he tried to explain the stark difference between two things that were very different.

Problem is, he couldn't find a suitable phrase to convey the thought.

Although there's plenty of words we can use to describe things that are similar, it turns out there weren't any to describe things that are different. To fix this, he coined a phrase that's still used today. He said that when describing two different things, they were like "chalk and cheese."

Memorize it.

Because it explains much about the relationship between kings (entrepreneurs) and the Church today.

We (entrepreneurs) couldn't be more different (from the church) in many ways.

And that's a problem.

But it's not our fault.

It's not your fault and it's not someone else's fault either.

Fault implies blame, and we're not blaming anyone here. Think of it more like being right-handed vs. left-handed.

If we're going to see explosive impact for Jesus in our communities, the only way the forgotten formula (Business + Mission = B.O.O.M. or Business Operating on Mission) works is if we can find a way to build a bridge between business and the Church. Just as we saw in the Old Testament. When the kings didn't do things on their own, they were supported by priests and prophets (or the ministry folks) who came alongside them.

The challenge today is how do we do this, because for centuries the Church has flipped the system on its head, so undoing that change is going to take a significant mindset change.

We're different.

It's not a cute catchphrase from an Apple ad, it's the truth.

And it applies to many, many levels.

We think differently about time, its value, and what can be accomplished.

We think differently about money, what it is, and what we're supposed to do with it.

We think differently about people, about culture, about pretty much everything in between.

We're wired with a hustle and drive that isn't typical.

With creativity, passion, and a desire to build things, *no matter the risk* (let's be honest, if we even do a risk assessment, we find a way to make those assessments say YES!).

We develop things and cultivate things at an incredible pace to help us identify what is or isn't working as efficiently as possible.

Because failure is good if we can do it quickly.

It shows us what not to do so we can refocus on a better way.

We don't work by committee. We often make decisions from our gut.

Perhaps the biggest difference of all is that when we have an idea or chase an idea, we put our money where our mouths are, because we're investing and taking risk with resources we own, control, and may lose.

Entrepreneurs start things and build things, often preferring to sell them and go do it all again rather than keep leading it once it grows. We thrive on it because we're wired to start stuff.

I think it's because we're like Jesus. He was a creator too. The universe. Tables. Who knows what else!

It's our strength, our skill, and our curse all at the same time.

Remember that, "risk" thing? Entrepreneurs really do have an appetite for risk that goes beyond the comfort level of most because you can't win big without betting big.

And boy do we bet.

But only in a spiritual way that makes Jesus happy.

Never in Vegas.

I pinky promise.

We have a singular focus that can come across as brash and direct. We're not trying to be, it's just how we're wired and being efficient with our words and speech saves us time.

Yes, we really do think about time down to the level of how many words are coming out of our mouths.

We have the patience of a black rhino (the least patient of all the animals in Simba's world) and want everything done now. To be fair, that's not just because we're impatient, but because building amazing things takes an amazing amount of our energy, life, and mental capacity. So, we don't have time to spare.

We also need to beat everyone else to the punch.

We're more successful if we do and can dominate our market.

Our minds run three steps ahead, analyzing situations, finding answers to problems others haven't seen, while thinking about the pressures and challenges we're facing.

None of these are bad things and no one needs to think it's their job to try and change them. We sure don't need anyone to try. We embrace them, lean into them, and enjoy the variety that God has created in human beings to deliver the different outcomes He desires.

I say all this because if you're an entrepreneur, I need to tell you something.

It's okay.

It's okay to be different.

Really.

It's more than okay to be different.

God made you that way.

Stop trying to be someone you're not.

Stop trying to look like someone else. Stop trying to operate outside your gifting.

Don't be a poor version of someone else when you can be the best version of you.

God isn't asking you to become a mini-me of your church leaders. He made you you for a reason.

Even Dr. Seuss figured that out.

If you're not an entrepreneur yet (!), maybe show us a little grace. You'll need it too one day. It doesn't matter if you're a church leader or our next-door neighbor. Your job isn't to change us. That's God's gig.

Could it be that some folks' way of seeing the world is different from the entrepreneur's perspective, like the right- and left-handed example, and that that is okay? You've realized that Jesus may not see the world the way you do all the time either, right? I know I did a long time ago.

The best thing you can do is support us and coach us from the sidelines if we need help.

In love.

Encouraging us to lean into our strengths on the field of Marketplace, cheering us on and praying for us often.

We need it.

We'll talk more about spiritual warfare in the next chapter but for now, it's important those around us understand there's a real Enemy who wants our businesses to fail just as much as he wants Jesus to fail.

In the past six years I've been involved in more lawsuits than I care for and one state investigation. Does that sound reasonable for a small business?

Welcome to club Mensa if you said no.

When these things happen, who notices?

My extended family didn't.

Most of my friends didn't either.

Neither did my pastor. He was fired up on Sunday mornings about the next conference, building campaign, or fundraising program while I was trying to figure out what on earth was happening.

Let's pretend for a second that someone notices the extra gray hairs and wrinkles under my eyes. What would they say? "Jesus has your back"?

If they did, I'd likely lay my sweet Jesus-loving hands on them.

And I don't mean in prayer.

I can figure out that Jesus has my back all by myself.

It's not a helpful statement when I'm in the middle of complete chaos.

Oftentimes today's churches are so focused on *their* mission, *their* purpose, and *their* issues that they miss the part about their mission being to serve everyone else's. We've demonstrated from Scripture that we're supposed to lead the charge, fund the work, and help bring life to it. That's our purpose and calling as believers who are all priests.

Even more so as entrepreneurs who God made to be kings.

Doesn't it make sense then that others around us help us win, because if we win, Jesus wins?

Did you notice the part where Jesus hung back and sent out the disciples to do the work while He was still here? Why do that when you're the MVP? Because the principle was the same then as it is now. He was there to grow them, not Himself.

Think about this.

The New Testament church had no buildings, almost no overhead, and minimal operating costs to speak of. Just a real-life, organic community that *all* participated in the mission of kingdom by living authentic, everyday lives and making Jesus the main thing in everything they did. Somehow, they managed to explode over the first couple hundred centuries with nothing more.

It started to slow down when buildings and institutions appeared because someone thought we should look like every other religion in the world for legitimacy, and we're still dealing with the consequences of those decisions today. Chalk and cheese.

God's kingdom functions best in the original model. The unorganized organization. Led by Him. In the same way that He wanted to lead Israel in the Old Testament but all they could do was look at everyone else and decide they needed a human king also.

What a crock.

They had the King of kings and wanted a downgrade because they couldn't see the bigger picture. Chalk and cheese.

Institutions and institutionalism never achieve anything great, meaningful, or lasting. Organic, grassroots groups do. That's why the organic first-century church was called *ekklesia* in the New Testament. That Greek word *always* referred to the body, the people, the priesthood of all believers and never to a building. They didn't have any.

People were empowered, supported, and encouraged *by each other* with a not-professional shepherd or coach by their side. Cheering them on. With no other motivation or agenda.

We see examples of the Old Testament kings in the New Testament. They're the ones who sold land and assets to share around the community, so nobody went without. We read about them in Luke's book called Acts.

They didn't do this because they were asked (there's no record of that). They did it because they were priests, following the voice of their favorite guy, Jesus. Wanting to be obedient, wanting to prove that love does, and love lives, while recognizing that their blessings placed them in a position to help where others couldn't.

So, they stepped up.

They didn't need someone to create an offering goal with a wall chart or crowdfunding campaign so they could watch the line grow. They didn't need to fund another building because no one was building any. They had homes and recognized the superiority of smaller community groups.

Settings that didn't just allow everyone to grow and develop their gifts, but actually encouraged and promoted it.

Today, our buildings point us at the front in an entertainment format. Back then, they sat in circles to engage with everyone. Chalk and cheese.

The original format worked better and yielded better results than our alternative format of today. It's why the small group / house church model is fashionable again. Because it worked then and works now.

As an entrepreneur I've been asked countless times to help some incredible causes and nonprofits in my local community and church. But I don't know if those same people have ever come alongside and asked with any meaning or depth what help *I* needed to fulfill God's call and mission in my kingdom (my business).

Their mission usually has people but needs funds.

My mission usually has funds and, because of that, people.

There's no evil plan to screw everything up, we're simply reaping the seeds sown of institutionalism, religion, and tradition. Leaders plan fundraising while announcing the next initiative they think God has shown them and expect everyone to fall in line as good Christian stewards of what God's blessed them with.

Translated, we should write another check and trust they know what they're doing.

Respectfully, don't do it.

They may be wrong.

God will speak to you about your focus area. Learn to ask and wait, patiently if needed.

It's okay you're feeling the way that you're feeling and asking the questions you're asking because something *is* wrong.

Very wrong.

And it needs to change.

Have you ever wanted something so badly, you just can't stop thinking about it, researching it, talking about it, or dreaming about it?

I was part of a small church once that had this problem.

The leadership team was fixated on buying up more land and building more buildings. Seems fair enough, you may be thinking. But they couldn't even fill the two services they already had.

Two.

What happened to three and four?

We hadn't even made it past two services on a Sunday, and they were ready to take on millions of dollars of debt to build bigger buildings, convinced God would fill them if they did.

Maybe they were Kevin Costner fans?

But I wasn't.

They were good people with good intentions but that's not enough. There was no way I could unite around that cause, and from an entrepreneurial perspective, it was crazy. Now, years later, the land sits empty, and the church hasn't grown. Except in debt. Wasting more of God's money.

In business, we use what we have until it's worn out before we commit more capital unless there's a safe bet on the horizon. We preserve cash as much as is fiscally appropriate, growing cautiously but carefully when the time is right.

I grow my businesses at the speed of cash because I don't think the Bible was joking about the whole debt thing and how it makes us slaves to its master.

Why don't churches do the same?

When church leaders chase whims, it proves their lack of ability in handling resources. And the "business" of church is rampant. It's so "normal" that leaders don't see the black holes they're walking into.

But we do.

You do.

I do.

Not out of judgment or nit-picking, but because our minds

are trained and developed to see things differently. Don't feel bad if you relate. It's chalk and cheese.

God made you that way.

He made me that way too.

We look for problems, for patterns, for efficiency. We ask tough questions and expect solid answers, not because we don't believe God is in something, but because we know ideas are like rear ends.

Everyone has one.

Some are better than others.

The ability to execute and deliver is a whole different story, and we want to see things that deliver. Until we know for sure they can deliver and will deliver, we just assume it's last night's pizza talking.

What if they got it wrong?

Everyone else pays the price.

When we get it wrong, we pay the price. You think differently when it's your money vs. someone else's. That's why so many startups chase capital from investors. They don't want to risk their own.

I remember a well-meaning preacher relaying to his audience that God told him he'd die on March 30 of that year if he didn't raise eight million dollars by the end of the month. When the date passed without hitting the goal, he said he'd misquoted, and meant to say by the end of the year, not the month.

Awkward.

I'm not debating his actions or his heart, but there's too many examples of things like this to convince successful entrepreneurs that we should blindly hand over resources when we're competent and capable and could use them ourselves either for kingdom work or our own.

Imagine telling a pro football player , "Go ahead and throw me that ball, I'll take it from here." Unless substances are involved, no quarterback on earth is giving you that ball. He's already doing his job with the tool he needs right there in his hand. Why would he pass it to you?

We've all seen those posts on social media about the things God's doing through so-and-so's ministry. Celebrating God's hand on someone's life and work is awesome. But how many times have you ever seen those same folks post about what God's doing in the lives of the entrepreneurs in their community?

In the lives of the business leaders in their church.

Doesn't God move outside the walls as well?

I think He does.

A lot.

So why not celebrate it?

Instead of another video post showing the band on stage. Entertaining. While everyone watches.

Can you imagine a coach doing the post-game interview but only talking about his own greatness while never referring to the players? If you can't, search YouTube for Jose Mourinho and watch. He does a pretty good job of it. Which is why no team keeps him around for more than a year or two.

In my whole life I've only ever seen a church leader get behind an entrepreneur in his church one time, on the stage, encouraging others to go check out his business. It was awesome.

But why only once?

What if they supported their entrepreneurs more, like when they're facing supernatural opposition, by praying and fasting specifically for them and those battles?

The model we have now isn't working. Churches, ministries, and nonprofit organizations can't handle the Great Commission by themselves. Two thousand years has proven that so, surely, it's time for a reboot?

We need to go back with Marty McFly and his DeLorean time machine.

All the way back to God's original design.

Jesus paved the way for all believers to be priests, to hear God's voice and communicate with Him, so isn't it only natural that He would speak into the lives of business leaders who operate and live on the playing field of Marketplace? The very place most unbelievers and hurting people can be found.

If you've been feeling a lack of purpose or disillusionment with the status quo, I get it.

There's a reason you're noticing things.

The Holy Spirit is trying to catch your attention.

That's His heart and hurt that you're feeling.

It's Him calling you to step up and do more.

If you've been feeling guilty because of your success in business, don't.

It's okay.

God blessed you that way for a reason.

We just need to unwrap the gift to find out what it was given for.

If you've been sensing your business might have more to offer than its core products and services, I'm here to cheer with you as you continue seeking God's heart. Because there is *so much more* He wants to do through your company, through your team, and through your capabilities.

It's not too late, you haven't missed anything.

You're right where you're supposed to be, and it's about to get interesting.

We've already talked about God having a marketplace-first perspective both in the garden of Eden (the very first book of the Bible) as well as through the life of Jesus (who was an entrepreneur first, miracle worker later). Now we need to go deeper, to understand in practical terms what this could look like for entrepreneurs moving forward, and how He placed a formula in Scripture for us to follow.

CHAPTER 7
NOT QUITE A LOVE LETTER

It was a Sunday night in September 1993. Me and "the boys" (a.k.a. a dangerous posse of teenage church kids with licenses to drive) heard about a youth event that was happening on some neutral turf close by. Given some of the group were on the lookout for girls, it seemed like a moment made in heaven was right in front of our eyes. We piled into a couple of cars and headed over like the T-Birds from *Grease*.

We didn't find any "Pink Ladies," but we sure did find gold!

It was a pretty big student event and there were plenty of folks we didn't know. The hunters turned on their radars as they scouted for prey.

I wasn't part of that group.

No seriously, hear me out.

Although some of my buddies were looking for dates, Andy and I (one of my closest friends from school) weren't that interested as we'd moved to a higher plane of enlightenment at the tender age of nineteen. When he realized he hadn't locked his amazing hot rod (I use the term loosely given it had no resemblance to the 1948 Ford Deluxe Convertible also known as "Greased Lightning" and cost him maybe $800) we snuck out mid-service to make sure no one had stolen it.

Turns out they hadn't, and it was right where we left it, although I'm still not sure whether Andy was relieved or disappointed at that moment. I felt cheated, given I'd had two cars stolen and he'd had none. One of mine was only worth $300, with a deductible that was $300, and I'd just spent $60 filling it up with gas, so I was negative on the deal.

By the time we got back, we'd missed a few parts of the night, but another buddy was raving about this cute girl who'd just been on stage. My radar still wasn't interested because his definition of cute and mine were usually pretty different, but hey, we wanted to be godly, supportive brothers in Jesus, so we agreed to hang out afterwards and support the cause. He warmed up his moves like a pro athlete getting ready on the sidelines, looking for the girl he'd seen just moments ago.

Then it happened.

Our "T-Birds" connected with the "Pink Ladies" and the conversation flowed like a water hose. I'm not sure where my mind was but it wasn't in the moment. I can't blame my phone as they weren't a thing yet, but whatever the reason, I just wasn't feeling *it*.

I was in a holy period of life like Samson, except he'd been told to consecrate himself whereas I got the idea all by myself, deciding that girls were a distraction because I was going to be consecrated to Jesus. Because of this, I'd gotten used to the idea that I was going to be single so I could be even holier.

A couple girls needed a ride home to a neighboring town that was just far enough away to make it a not-small ask. Feeling chivalrous, we did the right thing, offering them a ride because what would Jesus want us to do?

Take the pretty girls home, right?

Exactly.

The cutie that Steve was interested in was one of two who rode in my car. As the journey progressed, I began to realize my buddy might have been onto something, as she really was pretty amazing. I looked in my rearview mirror way too much, so I saw her, but wrestled internally as my buddy saw her first and called dibs.

I knew I had to honor the "bro" code and left it at that.

Over the next few months, the T-Birds and Pink Ladies stayed in touch using all available methods of the day. Carrier pigeons weren't great, and landline phones weren't much better as we were never home. Long story short, I found myself on the phone with Miss Cutie, accidentally setting up a date a few months later. Originally planned as a group night out but as people bailed, just the two of us were left. Nervous, I figured I'd make it a double date just in case she was crazy, and we went to the only place that mattered, a restaurant called Shezan.

Shezan was my happy place.

I was like a king in his castle because I went there way too often. It was like walking into an episode of *Cheers* where everybody really did know my name, my favorite table, my usual order, and more.

Like a mafia boss I would sit down and simply nod, as they took care of me, every time I stopped by. My logic was simple though. I couldn't live without Indian food so this was a test to see if there would ever be a second date.

If she didn't like the food, it was over.

I was leaving the next day for a 3-week ministry trip to India and wouldn't be back until the new year. Although I'd vowed to remain single for Jesus, I was beginning to wonder if that was a smart decision, so I did what we all do, and back-tracked in prayer. "Did I really hear your voice, Jesus, or was it the pizza talking?"

It was a simple prayer, nothing majestic or profound.

I needed to know if I'd made a mistake.

While overseas I had my first taste of real, spiritual battle in a country overwhelmingly not Christian. One day I was 'enjoying' Delhi belly (by enjoying I mean suffering in excruciating pain), the next I was running for my life while chased by crazed Hindu fundamentalists. I didn't think my preaching had been that bad, so it felt a little harsh to see them destroy the whole outdoor stage and start attacking everyone.

I returned home twenty pounds lighter thanks to the sickness and eager to see my new friend again.

I arrived home to a handful of love letters. Given the short trip, sending them to India didn't make a whole lot of sense.

Those letters changed everything.

Before even opening them, they told me a story.

They told me she'd been thinking about me, more than once. They told me that, maybe, God has enough of a sense of humor to answer a dumb prayer while winking in our direction. They told me that date number two was a double green light, and that even if she wasn't the "one," perhaps a life of solitude wasn't in my future.

Ultimately, they changed the direction of my life.

They caused me to re-evaluate the path I was on. A path I'd started on with the best intentions. A path I believed whole-heartedly was God's plan, because I was literally following Jesus' footsteps, staying single to avoid the distractions of dating. Those letters caused me to think beyond the false limits I'd created in my mind, to see a different future with a bigger picture.

This chapter is my letter to you, church, nonprofit, or ministry leader.

I love your heart.

I love what you're trying to do.

I love your hunger for Jesus and reaching people with His message of grace.

I love the sacrifice you've made as you've chased the dream of serving Him because I get it, you want to impact the world for Jesus, and you believe the course you've charted is a good one.

I really, really want to see you succeed, but I'm worried you might not.

Not because you aren't capable, but because you've gotten a little sidetracked without even realizing it.

If this isn't you, maybe it's for "a friend"? Seeing as you're already here, maybe carry on reading so this chapter can help them through you, *wink*.

Leading a spiritual group isn't easy. Whether it's a nonprofit, church, or para-church organization, some days are just tough. In fact, it can be really bad for your health.

Did you know:

- The average divorce rate among pastors in America is around 50 percent? So, one out of every two pastors' marriages will end in divorce (in other words, about the same percentage as everyone else).
- 50 percent of pastors are so discouraged they would leave the ministry if they could, but they don't because they feel as though they have no other way of making a living.
- 70 percent of pastors constantly fight depression.
- 80 percent of pastors' wives feel their spouse is overworked and wish he would choose another profession.
- The majority of pastors' wives surveyed said that the *most destructive* event that has occurred in their marriage and family was the day they entered the ministry.

The fact that you're fighting the fight and moving forward is incredible. You're beating the odds; your commitment is inspiring. With benefits like that, you'd think no one could ever make it as a church leader, but you're proving them wrong.

But have you ever wondered why so many of your peers are in this mess?

Is it possible that the role we've created in modern-day America is the problem?

Is it possible that the right people are in the wrong seats of the Team Jesus bus?

Hear me out for a moment. It's like Dorothy being in Kansas without the ruby-red slippers. She'd be the right person in the right place, yet missing a vital ingredient. I believe there's an ingredient missing today too.

Scripture outlines a formula that helps fuel the impact we're supposed to make in the world for Jesus, but it's been forgotten, overlooked, and occasionally, just plain ignored.

It's a simple formula that finds its roots in the Old Testament proverb: "one can slay a thousand but two can slay ten thousand." There's an exponential multiplication that happens when we combine certain elements, just like when you're watching fireworks explode on the Fourth of July. It turns out that any explosive needs both an oxidizing and a reducing agent to go *kaboom*. Each of those elements on their own are simply elements but when you put them together, wow, fun stuff happens.

The Great Commission is a reaction, the result of another combination of elements, but not the elements you might expect. I believe that:

Business + Mission = B.O.O.M.

You may be rocking the mission part.

You may be nailing it as you hustle each day at 100 m.p.h.

You may be seeing some really cool results.

But they're limited, restricted to the energy and efforts you and your team expend. You hustle harder, and see a little more success, but what you're really craving is the B.O.O.M., the place where the return is exponentially larger than the effort being put in. When putting in 1+1 ejects out 11 from the other side. It's the magic that takes addition, converts it to multiplication, and then makes an even bigger result than that.

If you've been wondering why it feels as though you're climbing uphill, without any time to break, you're not alone.

If you've been wondering how there's going to be enough of you to go around, when in reality there never will be, you're not alone.

You're like gunpowder.

Explosive and highly potent.

It's why I'm sitting here, cheering you on with my pom-poms waving as you walk onto the field and play each day. But gunpowder on its own isn't enough. It needs heat because it doesn't ignite until it hits over eight hundred degrees Fahrenheit.

The heat in your life might not come from inside a ministry bubble, because just maybe, you were created for a marketplace-first world too. Even though you felt the call, is it possible you answered it by sitting in the wrong seat?

What if you're an entrepreneur and not a ministry leader? What if you were built for business, which is why moving at the speed of committee isn't working for you?

Can those around you see it?

Have those around you spoken it out loud from time to time?

. . .

Your calling is absolutely to serve people, but maybe not in the institutions we've built.

You're too valuable to Jesus, to your community, and to the world to stay there. It's time to move out of the wrong role and into the right.

You wanted to help Jesus and live a life that shines for Him.

I get it.

I did too.

But some well-meaning folk or an incorrect theology has taken you down a road you weren't built for, shouldn't be on, and most of all, doesn't add the primer to ignite the powder that is God's plan for your life.

I'm also concerned about your health. Your mental and emotional health, because somewhere along the way God's original formula was flipped, so now you're carrying all the pressure, trying to lead everyone into the promised land like Moses.

But that's not how God designed it then, or now.

His leaders push others forward, from behind.

They help others lead *their* respective tribes and networks into the promised land.

They're servants of leaders. The kings, the entrepreneurs to whom He's speaking. The ones with the means and ability to pull off the Great Commission because they have a larger support system, capability system, and distributed skill set (across their employees) than you could hope for. And their team shows up five days every week. Sometimes more.

I believe God was serious when Jesus gave the Great Commission to go out and make disciples throughout the world and I believe He gave us a phenomenal formula of how to accomplish this in Scripture.

I believe God has unlimited funds to accomplish this goal, but have you noticed that He didn't give those funds to the local church?

It's by design.

If it wasn't, the world would already be saved, and we'd all be sipping mojitos with J.C.

Those funds are the primer, the igniter for your and my gunpowder. The thing that'll get us up to eight hundred degrees, and guess who has them, kings.

I've met some amazing church leaders with incredible street smarts. They've built some awesome things for Jesus through their razor-sharp focus. But that focus becomes an Achilles' heel. Reshaping church into something it was never meant to be. Creating a model that isn't sustainable or relevant in today's culture.

2020 proved that, not because the pandemic caused the change, but because it magnified the fact that change was necessary.

Church got sidetracked.

It changed from being the gas station, a pit stop for a believer's engine, into a profession. Ministry became a career path for young people who felt God's call tugging on their heart. We told people who wanted to serve God that the best way to do it is in the machine we've created, because we know best, and our church's goal is what matters.

Become an usher.

Volunteer.

The machine of Church needs to be refueled constantly, but the oil wells are running dry, and nobody's noticed.

We built an institution instead of a movement.

An entertainment venue instead of a life raft.

We're hanging out as though we're on a Caribbean cruise ship when in the distance the *Titanic* is sinking while all the people onboard drown.

We can't hear them; the band is too loud.

We can't see them, because we're all facing the stage, away from the hurting.

I know you've sensed it.

You've recognized the church Jesus set out to create wasn't confined geographically, locally, or racially. You've known in your heart that ministry has felt as though the engine's not running smoothly, as though a cylinder or two are misfiring. You're still on the road and headed the right way, but you want to go from thirty m.p.h. to one thousand m.p.h. and don't know how.

If you're wondering how we can fix this, I've got great news. It's super simple and starts with a single mind shift, where we flip back the priorities of our hearts and minds to align with God's plan all along.

It's time to re-evaluate the playing field of Marketplace.

Oh, and in case you were wondering, Miss Cutie was the one, still is the "one," and Shania Twain was kind enough to release a song about us a few years after that first date…it's called "You're Still the One."

CHAPTER 8
TWO SIMPLE RULES

Rule #1: Marketplace first.
Rule #2. Don't forget rule #1.

If you've ever watched a football game you've probably noticed that before the start, there's all kinds of people on the field, from coaches to players to camera crew and cheerleaders. Once the ref blows the whistle, however, everyone disappears.

Quickly.

The players separate themselves and stand ready to play the game. Everyone else stays off the field and finds their place on the bench or in the stands. Why? Because one group has the skills, energy, and desire to play. The others don't. It's why the most talented and gifted kids find their way to the draft and are rewarded with contracts to play professional football.

Something similar happened in the Church a while back when we flipped things on their head.

. . .

We started to think the most gifted and called should be encouraged to "serve Jesus" by joining the coaching staff vs. playing on the field.

The field of marketplace.

We made coaching the goal, coaching the profession instead of playing for love of the game. We convinced those who felt called to "ministry" that this meant the career ladder of Church, where their gifts were needed the most.

We had good intentions.

We wanted the Church to thrive.

We figured pulling the best, most talented folks onto the sidelines of coaching would help.

But it didn't.

It un-helped.

It weakened the Church's impact as we told our recruits that concerning themselves with money and "worldly stuff" wasn't important because loving and serving Jesus was enough.

Poppycock.

I heard this as a kid and believed it.

I chased the dream for years because everyone seemed to sing the same song. From the outside looking in, it seemed to make sense. I joined a church staff, not because I was the most gifted candidate, but, most probably, because I was the only candidate willing to apply for a role that paid so little.

My heart wanted to serve God, they needed help and the congregation expected that help to come through a "professional" vs. a volunteer.

I bought into the idea that loving Jesus would be enough.

But it wasn't.

Not for me, and it isn't for countless others.

If you've been around Church for a meaningful amount of time, then you know people just like me. People who tried the ministry thing and left. People who gave their all and were rewarded with food stamps. I went from making in a month to what I would then be making in a year. With a wife and three kids whose lives were suffering because I couldn't see the forest for the trees.

No one else could either.

I'm sure it helped a few folks in some small way, but what I needed was for someone to sit me down and help me see that the dynamite God put inside me could never explode because the primer was missing.

I'd moved out of a place of influence and success in the marketplace, and into the Church bubble of business.

It cost me years of my life. Time that could have been more effective for the kingdom had I stayed where God's favor rested.

But I didn't.

It created frustration and pain that could've been avoided.

My skills and abilities, my intellect and perspective were so different from the folks around me you might as well have put cheesecake on top of steak and wondered why it didn't taste right. We thought differently on pretty much everything and by the end, nobody was happy. Chalk and cheese.

Looking back, it's easy to see why.

They believed in a Church-first, everything-else-second model.

I believed in a marketplace-first, everything-else-second model.

We were wired completely differently.

Sound familiar?

If you're a coach, your job is to support, pray for, and guide (from a biblical perspective) the players on the field of the Marketplace. Just like Jesus, who did almost all his ministry and teaching *outside* the temple in the streets and towns.

The players, entrepreneurs, can't play the game effectively without that support because it's God's design.

If you're a player, then you're needed on the Marketplace field, every day of the week. You can't play the game from the sidelines because your influence there is limited and confined. That's okay because it's supposed to be. If it wasn't, and God intended for every coach to save the world and fix every problem, wouldn't it have happened by now?

If we look at the forgotten formula we introduced earlier, "Business + Mission = B.O.O.M.," we see that only by combining the two elements together does the ignition happen, providing a spark that creates an explosion for the kingdom.

We see leaders excited to encourage the most gifted and called to step into their destiny. A destiny in the Marketplace where they can create and build something God can bless. Those leaders can come alongside the players to see how they can help.

Who they'll pray for.

Who they'll counsel and give wisdom to.

Who they can lead, from behind, because someone smart once said that the one who is first should be last.

When they do that well, those players (entrepreneurs) will go on to create products and services as if they're doing it for Jesus.

They'll create jobs and environments that are better than the rest.

In case Jesus walks in and decides to work in one of them.

They'll create more impact and influence, while shining a DNA that's built on biblical principles and a biblical foundation, as opposed to empty words with no substance behind them.

They'll take the fruit and rewards of that blessing and *fuse* it with a mission to deliver the B.O.O.M. Jesus is looking for. On their own, it can work. Together, you can hit one thousand m.p.h. without breaking a sweat, changing lives along the way.

Jesus wasn't born a priest; He was born a businessman's son.

John the Baptist *was* born into a priestly family and ran off to the desert to get away from it as fast as he could.

Why?

So he could get closer to the people and be free to speak God's message into their lives.

It seems as though he didn't connect with the institution of the day.

Can't blame him.

Look at what they did.

Lying and sneaking around until they found a way to kill Jesus.

Today's generations with God's hand on their lives need to be told NOW, that God's calling is marketplace first. That calling is for the playing field, where business and relationship happens. Create a business or work in one, it doesn't matter, as long as you help one live out its God-ordained DNA.

Marketplace IS the ministry.

Marketplace *is* the ministry.

Marketplace is *the* ministry.

Repeat it like a mantra.

The calling so many of us feel wasn't to become another coach in the stands. It was to go out there and be a player on the field.

The field of Marketplace.

It's a field that isn't limited in size.

It's a field that doesn't limit the size of the team that can play on it.

It's a field that's like a potted plant getting ready to be placed into a bigger pot. It needs the room, so its roots aren't constricted.

Let's make the most of our youth, our energy, and our enthusiasm to get out into the marketplace, delivering influence and impact for Jesus.

While we're at it, let's make sure we encourage as many people as possible to do the same. Encouraging them to continue growing and developing, in the Marketplace, while surrounded by infinitely more people to reach with God's love than they would ever have if they limited their work inside the walls of the church.

We can't bring everyone to a church building because many people won't step foot in there. It's okay, the players can reach them, just like Jesus did.

Where one pastor can't be in a hundred different places at once, the players can.

Where one pastor can't be close enough to every hurting person in a community, to love on them and show them Jesus, guess what?

The players can.

That's the beauty of this distributed ministry model.

It's exciting to be alive at a point in history where God is pouring out an awareness of the power of business for His kingdom. Or maybe we're just more open to what He's been screaming from the rooftops for centuries.

It's incredible to see how He's bringing clarity and position to business leaders who are stepping into their calling and leading their kingdoms as God-appointed leaders. Supported and led by godly, spiritual coaches. Coaches who recognize that following the kings into their destiny IS fulfilling God's call, and not a distraction from their work in the church, or the work of the church (small *c*).

Coaches must recognize that these kings have communities of people they organically and naturally serve and reach. We could call them churches too.

They're just the same as any congregation.

Bodies of people being ministered to in the form of employees, customers, vendors, and partners.

As this Marketplace-first theology takes root, we need to empower it and fill it with the best we have to offer. The most gifted, the most talented, the most amazing people God has on Team Jesus.

. . .

We need to encourage and inspire the gifted and the called to see God's purpose and vision for business. To see how they can impact and shape a world around them, through the power of entrepreneurship and profit. We need to seize the day of small beginnings, recognizing that Apple, Microsoft, and Google all started with an idea between buddies, and nothing more.

We can stop the pain and losses for so many, before they travel the wrong road and experience the square-peg, round-hole syndrome others have lived through.

We can stop gifted people thinking it's their fault they don't fit in when it isn't. They were just in the wrong seat on the wrong bus.

We can surround them with great people, with great hearts and great intentions, who recognize their role is to support, pray for, and encourage these potential kings. Who recognize that wisdom and growth will come through the journey God has them on. We might not know the destination but that's okay, we just need to recognize the process.

Rather than trying to help in areas we don't need to, it could be more effective if we connected them with other entrepreneurs to learn from. Pointing them to wiser counsel from the Marketplace, as you cover them in prayer. If you're a coach, your job isn't to have all the answers, but to know where to find them.

Sometimes that's in other people.

Instead of hurting God's kingdom and the impact that *could* be witnessed in our world by removing gifted and talented people from the mission field of enterprise and business, let's find ways to put more there. That's the only way explosive impact for Jesus happens.

We think we're helping Jesus by bringing the gifted into ministry service, but we're really taking people away from a bigger calling.

What if they followed a different path and created the next Instagram? They could literally transform the lives of millions of people (all from a foundation of grace, love and positivity), while creating hundreds or thousands of good-quality jobs around that central hub.

Or they could teach Sunday school to a hundred people, half of whom haven't fully woken up yet on any given Sunday morning.

What if these kings could influence their employees by building out and living out a business model built on biblical foundations? They could take those profits (and the staff could take some of their wages) and fund projects that deliver impact, in resourceful and meaningful ways.

All of this is possible when we adopt a Marketplace-first theology and encourage those who feel called to serve Jesus in some way to push into their faith, and see IF that calling is to coach, or play.

The very gifts and competencies seen in others and wanted for God's kingdom were put there to achieve maximum impact.

Practically, maximum impact is more likely to happen outside the walls of church. Developing people in the fertile soil of the marketplace, of entrepreneurship and of business, makes more sense in light of that. This is where they can be surrounded by others who don't know Jesus and need to see their light shine the most.

Peter was a disciple of Jesus. He spent three years hanging out with Him pretty much all day and all night. He wrote a letter in the New Testament where he explains the concept of all believers being priests.

Theologians call it "the priesthood of all believers."

I know, super original.

In Peter's mind, he didn't think we needed to join the priesthood, or become priests by stepping into some type of role or position. He understood that if you believed in and followed Jesus then you automatically were one.

If anyone was qualified it was Peter. He'd spent years watching Jesus in everyday life.

Then there's Paul, the genius behind over half of the entire New Testament. Trained by the best (think Stanford or Harvard). Although he'd joined the coaching staff of the temple previously, everything changed when he met Jesus. He quit, choosing to play on the field, hitting the marketplace like a tsunami.

The real question is why?

If there was ever a coach to coach the coaches, it was Paul. No one was more qualified, smarter, more driven, or better placed influentially.

But he said no.

He recognized there was a *bigger* opportunity.

He could deliver greater influence and impact by choosing the Marketplace first. More than that, he recognized his entrepreneurial skills and capability. Capabilities that could be used to further the gospel and impact the kingdom.

Remember that part about it being more blessed to give than to receive? He meant it, so he put himself in a position that he could give from so he'd never need to receive.

In essence, he chose to leave the stands and walk onto the field.

Sure, he did a little coaching too, but isn't that what team captains do? Doesn't the quarterback direct and guide the players while they're out on the field, adjusting and adapting as necessary to advance and move forward?

Because of the choices this New Testament giant made, he was able to combine mission with business and deliver an explosive B.O.O.M. so big, it transformed the early church, and continues to transform our churches today.

His profits from "Paul and Co's Tentmaking" paid for himself and his entire entourage to travel the known world with the gospel. Instead of taking from the kingdom, he was giving back to it while at the same time being creative, just like his heavenly dad.

Have you ever wondered if his tents were any good?

I do.

And I don't even like camping.

As the guy who wrote that no matter what we do, we should do it as if we're doing it for Jesus, I'm thinking even his tents carried a special anointing like the handkerchiefs that healed people, but I digress.

•   •   •

I love the global Church and I love the local church, but there's no escaping our definitions aren't what were originally intended.

To reach and impact billions of people, we're at an inflexion point. The infrastructure that connects us and allows us to pour into so many people is owned through commerce and business. The talent pool is too strong for us to pull it out of the marketplace without weakening the impact of the gospel.

We need to strengthen it.

Because the world respects success.

Just look at Solomon's fame.

In my coworking business I've met and chatted with countless ex-preachers, ex-youth pastors and ex-children's pastors who've left the "ministry" and taken their God-given entrepreneurial heart to start something new. Building healthy businesses and generating profits while creating jobs.

Unfortunately, most of them never realized that the business they were building *was* their ministry and calling.

They never realized that God created them for *this* purpose. Instead, they carry the guilt and shame that comes when someone thinks they failed at their ministry calling, and as a result, failed Jesus.

You know what else?

Nobody told them that they're wrong for thinking that.

If this sounds like you, let's stop and have a micro-counseling moment. You *are* doing what God created you to do. You *are* being what God created you to be and you didn't fail at anything, you just took the long road to get here.

God's formula is for us to grow into kingdom "givers"

instead of "receivers" because everyone understands that too many receivers without enough givers spells disaster.

We need to take people's gifts and push them out to benefit everyone.

God doesn't just want but demands that we help the most gifted move into a position where they can achieve more.

By giving more.

Instead of spending more.

I don't mean giving more to a church but giving more to *the* Church by taking their gifts, abilities, and teams, and forging new paths of ministry through their business and entrepreneurial endeavors.

It's not about giving money; it's about giving something so much more valuable. You.

One way to do this is by delivering help and aid to others through self-sustaining, profitable projects. Run them like businesses instead of charities. But let the profits benefit those being helped and served because that's how it should be.

Read through an Old Testament book like Ruth and you'll see that God's law *required* harvesters, for example, to leave the leftover and spilled grain on the floor. Why? Because those scraps kept Ruth alive, and she happens to be part of Jesus' family tree.

Profits that vacuum up every last cent at the expense of others aren't healthy or biblical.

Profits that help others in multiple different ways are.

As we identify, nurture, and grow future entrepreneurs in a biblical way, they will go out and build companies that grow in influence and power. They will create great jobs and take care of their people. They will live out their faith surrounded by people watching, giving God's spirit an opportunity to work.

The gifts we recognize in people are real, but it's time to recognize that who benefits from those gifts is what really matters.

God didn't create us to be insular, looking inward while making some kind of Christian holiday camp. He needs us to take every fabric of our being and use it to benefit the world.

His world.

Those outside the church.

Could it be time for the organized Church to start working on shrinking its footprint, to retire its institutional mindset and grow its ministry impact by partnering and working with businesses and entrepreneurs? This upside-down kingdom where the head becomes the tail was God's idea anyway.

Could it be time for those gifted within church staff to recognize that those same gifts could be explosively more powerful on the field of marketplace?

Could it be time for us to recognize that the leaders in our churches who are truly gifted and called, are gifted and called to coach, cheer and support those playing on the field of marketplace, and shouldn't be left to try and do themselves what we should have been doing all along?

Instead of a mindset that says the Church needs to be doing everything, supported by the Marketplace, what if the Marketplace does everything, supported by the Church?

What if the Church had less staff, less leaders, and less buildings? We all know that means less expenses too. Yet we'd have *more* active ministers (you and me) delivering impact and more rewards.

What if by doing this we saw the body of believers feel more empowered and freer to step up? Growing into their giftings while recognizing their roles more clearly than ever before?

What if this resulted in a body of believers so strong in their faith that their communities would have to take note? So strong in their walk that the Enemy starts to sweat.

The model of "professionals" doing the work we're so used to seeing created the opposite of what's needed. Believers don't minister anymore. They don't reach out and they don't step out.

Why should they?

They're paying professionals to do that while they enjoy country club Christianity!

Are we really okay with that?

Did Jesus really die so we can buy a bigger boat?

God's kingdom demands more from us.

He demands more through business, through impact, and through sustainable, replicable growth. Through partnership and collaboration, instead of loneliness and isolation. Through a system that functions twenty-four hours each day, seven days each week.

I prophesy that a new day is here. A day for God's kingdom to succeed like never before. A day where we will experience a seismic shift for Jesus in our communities and our world.

But we're going to need to engage entrepreneurs and businesses like we've never engaged them before. We're going to have to recognize their leadership and calling to help take the gospel to the world.

We're going to need to accept the priesthood of *all* believers and accept that God is leading and speaking to them directly. That He's speaking to them independently of anyone else.

Change is coming. And it's going to be amazing! But someone's trying to stop it. An opponent, who also plays on the same field. The biggest, baddest, strongest opponent we'll ever meet.

CHAPTER 9
MR. BULLY

It was possibly the most perfect roundhouse I'd ever witnessed. You know what I'm talking about. The kind of kick that would have made Mr. Miyagi proud, and easily as impressive as Daniel-san's "Crane" at the end of *The Karate Kid* movie.

Even better than that, I wasn't on the receiving end of it! It was Craig, he was the lucky guy feeling the impact, the schoolyard bully, the bane of middle school existence.

You know a Craig, don't you?

We *all* know a Craig.

The arrogant chap, the cocky little so-and-so who's always looking to pick a fight, while secretly hoping no one ever stands up to him.

While I knew enough to appreciate the aerial acrobatics of that roundhouse kick, I also knew Craig was bad news. At twelve years old, I was no Dr. Phil or Oprah, but I knew enough to know Craig was someone I didn't need to be buddies with. Seeing him laid out on that school playground proved my point.

But we didn't arrive here without a little prequel action. Craig didn't just lay himself out on the playground that summer's day donning his best theatrical performance ever.

He'd made a mistake.

A big mistake.

You might say it was the boo-boo he'd never recover from in his career as my middle school John Gotti.

You see he'd become so comfortable, so confident in everyone backing down, that when he chose his last victim, his lack of recon, as they say in the military, was unforgivable.

We'll call the other guy *The Kid*, because it's a cool title and I don't remember his real name. Okay, I do and I'm lying, but I don't want him to suddenly get thousands of Facebook messages congratulating him on something that happened decades ago.

I looked him up and he's now some kind of legit martial arts ninja with a black belt, black costume, and probably a disguise to go with it judging by the photos.

The Kid was from a well-off family, and his folks knew no boundaries when it came to giving him what he wanted. He mastered everything he attempted and seemed to never get sidetracked.

He was that guy.

When he wanted to learn the guitar, while the rest of us were self-learning from magazines and books (pre-YouTube, folks, give me a little love here), his parents bought him a couple of serious *axes* (what we hip guitar players call them) and signed him up with a tutor who I swear used to play in a real life rock 'n' roll band.

Thanks to *The Kid*'s natural talent and determination, he was rocking that guitar like Slash from Guns N' Roses in no time.

Slash.

As in "Sweet Child O' Mine."

Not bad for a twelve-year-old.

Had strumming the six-string been the extent of *The Kid*'s interest, Craig might've gone home victorious once again, another victim notched into his belt. But he didn't, because it turns out *The Kid* was better at martial arts than he was at guitar, and that roundhouse he played across Craig's head sounded pretty sweet as it rang.

When the bullying started, *The Kid* showed more patience and discipline than most twelve-year-old boys, calmly suggesting Craig drop it and leave him alone. Showing his IQ for all to see, Craig missed those cues and didn't take the hint.

Even as *The Kid* changed his tune—and his stance—Craig continued the verbal diarrhea aimed his way. Seconds later, so quick you'd have missed it if you blinked, *The Kid*'s feet were spread wide, hands lifted up, and it was clear that he wasn't in the mood to play. One final act of bullying from Craig invited the infamous roundhouse kick that would become part of grade school legend and lore.

Our hero humbly walked away without looking back at the crumpled Craig left moaning in his own demise. The sweet sound of cheering youth ringing in his ears. It was a lesson I recall even today.

Force was the only thing Craig understood, and while I'm not a fan of violence, it sure solved the problem that day.

I still have a Craig in my life today.

You do too.

Only now he goes by a different name.

He's a bully who constantly harasses me, thinking he's safe because he's bigger and smarter than I am. Sometimes he's so obvious I can see it a mile away, but most of the time his ninja skills hide him really well, disguising his handiwork as something else or someone else.

Evil With a Capital *D* Spells Devil.

We barely start reading the first book of the Bible, Genesis, without humans being sidetracked by someone who would go on to be our truest enemy. His nickname, the Father of Lies, is fitting and probably one of the reasons the Bible says that God *hates* lying. I think that means He hates where lies come from too, and lying originated with the Devil, who was created by God but chose to rebel against Him.

Have you ever noticed that nowhere in the Bible does God say He hates murder even though He tells us not to do it? But lying is something God explicitly hates.

Huh.

The Devil was a bully in the beginning, and he continues to be a bully today. That same Devil who appeared to Eve in God's creation story, and immediately persuaded her to do something she shouldn't.

He's the master sidetracker.

. . .

He'll find just the thing to take your eyes off where they're supposed to be focusing and help you point them to where they shouldn't be.

Because he's the master accuser, he accused God of not having Eve's best interests at heart when God gave her a boundary she wasn't meant to cross. We all know how that forbidden fruit turned out.

Satan didn't just hang out in the Old Testament's garden of Eden until he decided to toss your life into chaos. He's been busy throughout history, honing his craft and fine-tuning his skills. Ever heard of the bloke named Judas? Yeah, not a fondly remembered member of Jesus' original band of merry men, but John tells us that it was Satan who entered Judas' heart (John 13:27).

It seems almost too easy to pick on him though, so let's head a little later, to the New Testament powerhouse, Paul. The Bible tells us his work was also hindered by Mr. Bully, when he wanted to travel to Thessalonica.

What about Job, whose book tells us Satan roams through the earth looking for people to harm?

How about Jesus, who describes him in John chapter 8 as *"A murderer from the beginning, and* [he] *has nothing to do with the truth, because there is no truth in him. When he lies, he speaks out of his own character, for he is a liar and the father of lies."*?

As we run through the Bible, we find so many examples of an enemy intentionally at work against God's people that at some point, unless we want to be like Craig, we just can't over-look or ignore them.

He spends his time roaming.

He spends his time looking for people to harass (like a typical bully).

He's a liar, a thief, and a deceiver (think Loki on steroids) and he'll do whatever he can to distract, prevent, or hinder any progress toward God's will or His kingdom.

To make things a little spicier, and because he's been doing this for thousands of years, it turns out that he's really really good at it.

Freaked out yet?

It gets worse.

He's not alone.

He has an army that helps him to make sure he's as successful as he can possibly be.

Do you remember that time Jesus said, *"whoever isn't for me is against me"*? (Matthew 12) I sure don't see fifty shades of gray in there, do you? If there's no middle ground then when you think about the Devil wanting to steal and destroy, what do you think that's referring to?

Your home?
Your car?
Your job?
Your life?
All of the above.

Some of us think in materialistic or possessive terms, because culturally, those are things we place value on and that causes us to translate verses like this to mean he wants to steal our "stuff," to make our lives less enjoyable.

But there's another layer he attacks because nothing short of total domination is good enough for him.

Mr. Bully wants to steal your joy, happiness, time, attention, and focus. He wants your mental health. He wants your actual health. He'll work through culture and entertainment to pull you into *anything* that takes your mind, heart, and focus off Jesus and His mission.

If it's politics, he'll suck you into debate.

If it's movies, the allure of Netflix, HBO, and Amazon Prime will keep you busy for every minute of the next eighty years of your life.

He knows which buttons to press, and he'll press them constantly, because he wants to win at making you lose.

If you're wondering why this is happening to you, don't. It's not just you. We all wonder, we all feel the frustration, and we all experience the hardships that come along with his efforts and work. But there's nowhere you can run and there's nowhere you can hide that's going to stop him or change it.

The bullying happens because we're in a battle.

Not just people who believe in Jesus.

All people.

Everyone, everywhere.

It's a battle of cosmic proportions that's been raging since creation and will continue long after we die, until Jesus returns and finishes the job He started on the cross two thousand years ago.

I'm not trying to scare you or turn into a holy roller that thinks it's the Devil's fault Walmart was sold out of baked beans today when you needed a can. But there is a balanced amount of awareness we need to have, and even more awareness is needed if we're seriously interested in making changes to our lives that benefit God's kingdom.

If those changes are focused on furthering God's mission by committing every resource we have to it, then we just grew the bullseye on our back exponentially bigger. We need to be aware of Satan's efforts because this battle is going to impact us more than anyone else.

Exciting, right?

Have you ever done something you felt so sure about, that felt so right you just knew you were put on this earth to do it?

I have.

Or so I thought.

In 2015, I opened my first coworking space.

We called it WorkLodge.

We'd been noodling on the idea for around eighteen months, the last six of which had been construction. During the planning stages we decided we wanted to do something different with the business, to use it as a catalyst and fuel for change that would impact our local community and beyond. To help achieve this we created a nonprofit organization (www.ft5k.org) so we could fund mission and kingdom work, through the profits of WorkLodge.

It was our first step in applying the forgotten formula "Business + Mission = B.O.O.M." for Jesus.

Boy, were we pumped.

On June 23 we officially threw open the doors and it was awesome.

No, really.

We'd been blessed with two sisters who joined the team and were both rock stars. I wish they were still here to see what they helped start.

A local, respected business leader with a heart for mission (thanks "Mattress Mack") came to speak for us and we were beyond excited at this new venture we'd created. It was going to change how people worked (for the better) as well as change how our business worked, through this unique relationship that fueled our nonprofit with profit.

We thought we'd cracked the code.

Until something else cracked.

It was December 23, six months to the day since that launch event, and we were getting ready to close for the Christmas holiday. A group were scheduled to visit who were interested in what was then our largest, team-sized office space. The owners had already visited and were bringing their team so everyone could see the new office they were hoping to move into. Our excitement was through the roof as we thought about our biggest deal to date.

But then we got sidetracked.

As we prepared to make everything look perfect, one of my team and I popped into the office to stage it perfectly for the arriving guests. She slipped off her heels to make it a little easier and with two hours to go, we discovered a problem.

"Why is the carpet wet?" she asked.

Never a good question no matter when it gets asked.

I was dumbfounded.

We're an office space so we didn't use water like other businesses might and besides, the restrooms were a *long* way from the office we were standing in. I don't know if I thought she was just teasing the first time she asked, but within thirty seconds I realized this wasn't a drill. I reached down, touched the floor, and sure enough, it was soaked.

After investigation, we found the water had somehow entered our space through the wall of an adjacent business. We lost the deal and instead of counting money in, we started counting money out as we dealt with the expense of getting things fixed.

On December 23.

Merry Christmas.

A few weeks later everything was back to new. We'd replaced flooring in a few offices, blown through thousands of dollars, but all was well, and we were officially back in business.

Except we weren't.

In late February it happened again.

Only this time it wasn't a few offices, it was more like six or seven.

Some of the spaces that flooded were occupied by paying members.

Ugh.

Instead of receiving monthly payments that were allocated to fund our nonprofit, we were back to fighting the effects of extensive water damage, tearing out flooring, drywall and more, piece by piece.

Staying laser focused on sales and growing our baby business was getting tougher, but by late April we were back in business again, locked and loaded, firing on all cylinders. What could go wrong?

Everything was like new, and we were selling more each month than we'd ever sold before. Double-digit units moved month after month leaving us feeling pumped. I basked, just a little, in the realization I'd proved the doubters wrong. The folks who thought I was crazy to build over a hundred private offices, *plus* co-working in a retail center, with zero experience in commercial real estate.

They were going to see God's faithfulness in action.

Because I'd said all along it was His idea to begin with.

Life was good.

No. It was amazing.

Then June happened...

It was a normal Sunday morning when I woke and began my usual routine. It takes me a while before I touch my phone in the mornings but when I did, the jolt of a missed call and voicemail from 6 a.m. got my attention fast.

Guess who it was from.

The owner of the business next to mine.

You know, the one who'd flooded my space twice in the last six months.

He'd never called before.

My heart sank.

I didn't know for sure there was a problem, but let's be honest, do you ever get calls at 6 a.m. on a Sunday to say hello?

Neither do I.

I'll never forget the words I heard: "Hi, Mike, this is Joe. You might want to head into WorkLodge and take a look around. We walked in this morning and our space is **underwater**."

I had no idea what underwater meant but I knew it couldn't be good.

It's not like the whole building could be twenty-five feet under, but it sure sounded worse than the last two times. I couldn't believe it. We weren't even a year old and here we were being hit again. This time, it qualified as a major catastrophe.

If that wasn't crazy enough, we were still trying to figure out how to pay for catastrophes one and two.

I got dressed and jumped in my truck (what else would I drive in Texas?). As I headed over, thoughts racing through my mind, I found myself thinking through multiple scenarios.

How much water was there?

How much space did it affect?

What were we going to do?

Would we even make it through?

We had no investors, no deep pockets to lean on. Just Linda, me, and the kids' piggy banks. Which we'd already run dry starting the business. But don't tell them, they didn't get any stock options.

I walked into the space like Peter stepping out to walk on water, tiptoeing around as if that was going to change a thing. It took less than five seconds for me to notice the wood floors warping and buckling from the moisture.

Yep, underwater.

There's no other way to describe it.

We'd been hit big time on this one and I knew it.

I started counting offices as I walked around. 1, 2, 4, 6, 10, 15, 20. It didn't stop. I kept walking and counting, rounding out at 39 impacted offices of various sizes.

I called my team, who were amazing. Tim's mom even came down to help on this one!

They rolled in as fast as they could to start helping with damage control. I don't know that I really stopped to ask them how *they* felt, we all just stood there for a moment in disbelief. Many of the offices were occupied, so our first course of action was to move those businesses to new, unoccupied spaces.

If you're wondering how that would affect our available inventory kudos, so was I. The water took out two spaces for each one affected because we lost the one underwater and the replacement office was now unsellable, due to the temporary coverage it provided for the folks we moved into it.

The restoration teams arrived and got to work. Sucking up water, cutting out drywall, and pulling up floors as we continued moving furniture and belongings. I had to make sure that when our members walked in on Monday morning, their day wouldn't be impacted because that's the level of service we'd promised them.

I also needed to salvage as much of our furniture as possible because we had no money to buy more.

If you've never seen a WorkLodge, you should know they're pretty amazing. Think if Mercedes-Benz made flexible office space and you'll be close. Even now, years later, people still walk in and the first word they say is "wow."

We were happy to aim for the moon because we were committed to building a business that served everyone as if they were Jesus, which meant delivering excellence was the only option.

I didn't flip out, keeping my cool despite the pressure.

But then my super-deluxe insurance policy turned out to be more of a McJunior. Apparently, insurance companies like to write policies with a zillion exclusions.

Who knew?

Despite assurances from my agent that all was okay, it wasn't.

Apparently, the water coverage part didn't cover water if it originated outside of our space. In their "pass the buck" business motto, the other business was liable.

"No worries, I'll tell the other guy's adjusters while they're here," I said. Friendly guys, who committed to absolutely zero while we were speaking, with our shoes half covered in water.

They continued this incredible silent treatment for the next three years.

Immediately, sales died.

We sold less office space over the next three months while the repairs were being made than the number of porterhouse steaks a squirrel can eat.

Not quite zero but as good as.

The contractors worked through the night, every night to minimize the impact and my rock star staff member Tim (with the awesome mom), changed his work hours to help. He'd come in through the night for cleanup as others worked, go home for a break, and then be back at 5 a.m. to make sure we delivered the exceptional experience we promised to our members. It's one of our guiding principles as a business, and Tim lived it out big time.

Most people handled it pretty well, but there were a few that didn't.

I didn't blame them, but I sure wish they could have been just a little more gracious. It's not like I caused the problem.

I remember a conversation with my landlord during this time where he jokingly commented that whichever gods I'd ticked off in some way must surely be done by now. I knew enough to know this wasn't the case, but it was prescient that even he could see a spiritual element to the drama.

My mind had so many questions. It just couldn't be normal for a brand-new, faith-based business that was created to fund mission and kingdom work to experience this level of attack. We were tiny. A blip on the radar of earth with no outside funding or backers. In my mind, we were nobodies from a spiritual perspective, so why all the turmoil?

Was it the Devil?

Was this a spiritual attack after all?

Should I have seen this coming after #1 and #2 and somehow stopped it through the power of prayer?

Was it just a coincidence?

Maybe. Maybe not.

I asked all kinds of questions but had very few answers. I started to doubt, wondering what I'd done in starting the business. I started looking inward, wondering if some sin was to blame. Something I'd done that moved me out of God's blessing.

• • •

Looking back, it was in this moment that I should have prayed like Elisha and asked God to *"open my eyes"* (2 Kings 6:17), fully expecting to see what's happening in the unseen realm.

What I know for sure is that God didn't cause it, and according to Jesus, if something isn't for me, it's against me.

With that in mind, I concluded that if it wasn't helping propel me *toward* the kingdom, then it had to be trying to pull me *away*. Which meant our old not-friend, Mr. Bully, was back in town.

CHAPTER 10
SPIRITUAL WARFARE

Do you love Jesus?

Have you chosen to follow Him and walk with Him?

Whether you answered yes or no, brace yourself because Mr. Bully doesn't care, he's coming for you. He's coming for everyone. No matter who they are or what they believe, because his goal is to hurt God and hurting people is the only way he can do that, because he knows how much God loves us.

This war we're in isn't optional.

It's real and it's happening.

Here. There. Everywhere.

Whether we choose to battle or not.

Paul was a genius. If we knew his IQ, it would probably be Mensa level. He wrote much of the New Testament and was a theological smarty-pants compared to his peers. His professor was Gamaliel, an Einstein of his day, yet Paul experienced a life of amazing milestones. Beaten to (almost) death multiple times and yet continuing his mission regardless.

When he wrote to his church in Ephesus, he taught them: *"we don't battle against flesh and blood, but against the rulers, against the authorities...against the spiritual forces of evil in the heavens"* (Ephesians 6:12).

We don't tend to dwell on verses that speak of battling, because here in America we look for the good. We're optimists. We love happy endings.

But.

On this subject, we have to pay attention. Our destiny and eternity literally depend on it.

Elisha was bald.

I like to think he's my twin from another mother although I haven't raised anyone from the dead like he did yet.

I'm working on it though.

When it happens, I'll post it on YouTube, TikTok, and everywhere else I can find.

We're introduced to Elisha in the Old Testament (2 Kings 6), in the year 851 BC, as he's dealing with a bully too, the king of Aram, who is picking a fight with Israel because Israel was God's favorite.

Every time Aram would make plans to attack or ambush the Israelite troops, God would speak to Elisha who'd pass the message along to the king of Israel. Armed with this supernatural intelligence, gathered by a swarm of heavenly drones and completely accurate, Israel would be ready and waiting for each attack.

Baffled and puzzled, the Arameans somehow connected the dots, realizing Elisha was the link. This one godly man was stopping them from winning.

He had to go.

They sent troops to capture him.

A lot of troops.

Enough horses and chariots to surround an entire city! But would it be enough?

Turns out Elisha didn't just have God's personal cell number on speed dial. He was the Tom Brady of his day in all things prophetic. An old school, Old Testament prophet. Not only speaking crazy words that didn't come to pass until years later, but doing the undoable, like raising the dead before Jesus did.

He woke up that morning much like I woke up on *that* Sunday morning, except he handled his day a little differently.

"When Gehazi, the servant of the man of God got up and went out early the next morning, an army with horses and chariots had surrounded the city. 'Oh no, my lord! What shall we do?' the servant asked.

*'Don't be afraid,' the prophet answered. 'Those who are with us are more than those who are with them.' And Elisha prayed, 'Open his eyes, Lord, so that he may see.' Then the Lord opened the servant's eyes, and he looked and saw the hills full of horses and **chariots of fire all around Elisha**"* (2 Kings 6:15–17).

The little bully thought he'd send his army out to harm Elisha, and just like Mr. Big Bully, he learned how inferior they were to God's power real quick.

Elisha had already seen his rescuer, but his helper hadn't. *"Open his eyes"* we read, and God doesn't show up, because

He's already there. We're given a glimpse of an unseen realm that had been invisible until that point. Even though he was surrounded in the physical realm, Elisha understood that we exist in a hybrid of two intersecting realms that collide.

Not realms like the Marvel movies, but realms, nevertheless.

The Aramean army thought they had this.

God's army had other ideas.

We see more than a few key principles here that translate across time and are helpful for us today, as we think about Mr. Bully and his workforce:

1. **B**efore God speaks, Satan is listening so he can find a way to stop what God wants.
2. **U**nderstanding God's will and calling on our lives better than we do, the Enemy will work to stop us.
3. Listening to the Holy Spirit when we find ourselves in situations that overwhelm us will bring us peace and show us how God will rescue us.
4. Looking at the Enemy isn't helpful. Looking beyond him to see God at work is the key.
5. **Y**ou will be surrounded. You will come under attack, but when that happens, God's protection will already be there. To protect you. Specifically. Guaranteed. Because He promised it.

Understanding the connection between Satan, spiritual warfare, and Jesus is critical not just in relation to successful living, but also in relation to our spiritual growth.

Jesus showed us another example when He walked the earth.

The Temptations. Not the Singing Ones.

"He will command his angels concerning you, to protect you."

King David wrote that verse in the book of Psalms, as one of the many worship songs he sang to God.

But that's not why we know it, is it?

We know it because the Devil made it famous.

When he quoted it.

To Jesus.

It happened right after Jesus burst onto the scene and was baptized by His cousin John. He went off into the desert for some quiet time with His dad, praying and fasting for forty days. It was during this time we're told that Mr. Bully showed up.

Just like in the garden of Eden.

When Adam and Eve were kicking around.

He rolled into town eager to try those same tricks one more time as he tried to sidetrack Jesus and shift His focus away from God. Jesus, however, knew how to respond. With Scripture. Neutralizing the attack.

So, Mr. Bully did something crazy, quoting Scripture back.

That's right, apparently, he knows the Bible pretty well.

Maybe better than we do.

He quoted the Scripture above, the one about God protecting us with His angels. Right before asking Jesus to try and harm Himself. Today, he'd probably play a game of Russian roulette, but the edge of a cliff was all they had back then.

Thankfully, Jesus knew a bigger and better Scripture that overruled this one, and the rest, as they say, is history.

Knowing what God's Word says isn't enough.

We've got to know what it says, in relation to itself as well as in relation to us. If one verse supersedes another, we need to know that and why, so we aren't pinning our hopes on something that doesn't apply. This is what Paul tried to explain to us in his concept called "the armor of God" in the New Testament. In his letter to the church in Ephesus he comforts all believers by explaining that God has provided weapons and protection to help us on our journey of life. We wouldn't need armor to wear if we weren't going into battle, would we?

Let's look at a couple of popular translations to help us get a grasp of what Paul is speaking about:

New International Version: Ephesians 6	The Passion Translation: Ephesians 6
11 Put on the full armor of God, so that you can take your stand against the devil's schemes.	11 Put on God's complete set of armor provided for us, so that you will be protected as you fight against the evil strategies of the accuser!
12 For our struggle is not against flesh and blood, but against the rulers, against the authorities, against the powers of this dark world and against the spiritual forces of evil in the heavenly realms.	12 Your hand-to-hand combat is not with human beings, but with the highest principalities and authorities operating in rebellion under the heavenly realms. For they are a powerful class of demon-gods and evil spirits that hold this dark world in bondage.
13 Therefore put on the full armor of God, so that when the day of evil comes, you may be able to stand your ground, and after you have done everything, to stand.	13 Because of this, you must wear all the armor that God provides so you're protected as you confront the slanderer, for you are destined for all things and will rise victorious.
14 Stand firm then, with the belt of truth buckled around your waist, with the breastplate of righteousness in place,	14 Put on truth as a belt to strengthen you to stand in triumph. Put on holiness as the protective armor that covers your heart.

15 and with your feet fitted with the readiness that comes from the gospel of peace.	15 Stand on your feet alert, then you'll always be ready to share the blessings of peace.
16 In addition to all this, take up the shield of faith, with which you can extinguish all the flaming arrows of the evil one.	16 In every battle, take faith as your wrap-around shield, for it is able to extinguish the blazing arrows coming at you from the Evil One
17 Take the helmet of salvation and the sword of the Spirit, which is the word of God.	17 Embrace the power of salvation's full deliverance, like a helmet to protect your thoughts from lies. And take the mighty razor-sharp Spirit-sword of the spoken Word of God.

The passage finishes by telling us to pray on all occasions, with all kinds of prayers. In other words, no matter what you're feeling, prayer is the ultimate antidote to the Enemy's poison. Let's look at four key concepts that should encourage us from this passage, that will strengthen our faith and give us boldness:

1. We can't and won't be protected without God's armor, so we need to understand this passage.

God knew there'd be times we'd be scared. He knew there would be times we'd be attacked, surrounded, overwhelmed, and hearing the voice of doubt. To help us, He provided the ultimate PPE (personal protective equipment). The "armor of God" gives us confidence that everything will be okay. We don't have to run scared, shirk our responsibilities, or feel exhausted and frustrated when things come against us.

The obstacles in the road *are* the journey.

He saw them ahead of time.

They aren't a surprise to Him so don't try to go around them. Go through, go over, but never sidestep. That's how we overcome and gain victory, just like Jesus when death thought it had Him. It didn't, God had death surrounded.

2. We aren't battling people. We're battling "powers of the dark world," "demon-gods," and "spiritual forces" in the heavenly realm.

Don't pray against people. Don't get angry at people. They're not the Enemy. They're just being used by him.

When challenges and pressures come through others, remember it's not really them that wants you to fail, it's the Enemy behind them. He's the Father of Lies, so every lie in some way originates from him, his energy, his influence, his *something*. I don't know *how* it works and I can't explain the details, but I do know he can get in anybody's head and heart. He's proved that consistently over thousands of years.

Our confidence is in a God who's already dealt with him.

We don't need to get caught up in any crazy rituals but can simply stick to the principles God communicated to us by humbling ourselves and standing strong. The Bible tells us demons will know our names, which means you're on their radar.

It's okay, they were on God's radar first.

3. We're playing defense.

The armor helps us stand our ground, not take ground.

We're playing defense while God plays the offense to advance His kingdom. We don't go looking for trouble, but we're ready to deal with it when trouble shows up. We focus and fix our eyes on His kingdom, seeking God as Jesus taught us through the Lord's Prayer. When we honor Him and obey Him, we can stand our ground when the attacks come, confident that God will work *"all things for the good of those that love him"* (Romans 8:28).

4. Our armor includes truth, righteousness, the gospel, faith, God's Word, prayer, and salvation.

Individually, the pieces are unique. Collectively, they're dynamite. They give us everything we need. The shield of faith for protection means that when those attacks come (the fiery darts), we can stand on our faith to *defend* ourselves, while speaking out in faith to *protect* ourselves.

· · ·

The helmet of salvation is most significant, because protecting our heads and minds is everything. We receive salvation from the work Jesus completed through His death on the cross which defeated death, Satan, and everything in between.

Salvation was given because Jesus died in my place and yours, that's how we ride those victory coattails. It's also why the battle that's raging for our hearts and minds is so crucial, because if we lose the mind battle, the heart and everything else follows. In the words of Journey, "Don't stop believing." Ever.

Have you ever had that feeling when your mouth is moving, and sounds are coming out of it, but your brain is saying stop? Peter had one of those moments, while talking to Jesus.

They'd just finished a big feast at the local diner, when Jesus took one last opportunity to explain to His peeps that He was about to die but it was all going to be okay because that's how He would triumph over death. In fairness to Peter, I think most of us would have had the same response. *"No way! That's a terrible idea."* This ideation stage is key because we know a few critical details about Peter that we shouldn't overlook:

1. Peter was a Christian, part of Jesus' inner circle, who would go on to be the first gospel preacher.
2. Peter loved Jesus.
3. Peter was you and me.

The heart of Peter's concern about Jesus' death wasn't what it seemed. The idea of Jesus not fulfilling God's ultimate calling on His life went against everything Jesus stood for and an idea like that couldn't have originated in Peter's mind, that concept, that idea could only originate from someone *against* God's will and purpose. Satan.

No, Peter wasn't possessed by the Devil. It's more like some type of nuanced way that Satan was able to drop an idea, a concept, into the energy of the room that Peter was able to pick up on. It wasn't concern for Jesus' well-being, even though it appeared that way on the surface. It was about the kingdom remaining first, and our desires second. It wasn't a bad thing that Peter didn't want Jesus to suffer, but God needed Jesus to die so that Jesus could defeat death.

That's why Jesus bypasses Peter when He responds to Mr. Bully:

"Jesus turned and said to Peter, 'Get behind me, Satan! You are a stumbling block to me; you do not have in mind the concerns of God, but merely human concerns'"–(Matthew 16:23).

Is spiritual warfare real? Absolutely.

Do I understand it even remotely enough? Absolutely not.

Does God win in the end? Absolutely.

If you remember those takeaways more than whether we agree or disagree on some of the details, my work here is done.

Collectively, we can agree that there is an unseen realm. It's real, it will affect us, so we need to be ready for it. I couldn't write a book about God's desire for your business to be rocket fuel for His kingdom without warning you of the road ahead.

During the difficult times you'll hear the doubts.

I did and still do.

During the difficult times I wonder if I really heard from God at all. If He really said what I thought He said.

I've learned that it's okay.

It's normal and it's human.

The key is to move on, and refocus not on what you're feeling, or what you're thinking, as they're both subjective and highly emotional. Focus on what God is saying, and did say, in His Word. It hasn't changed and never will. It's complete and true and happens to be the only offensive weapon in the armor God provided for His children.

Interesting.

When you choose to re-evaluate how you view your business, in light of God's mission and kingdom, taking up the challenge to live like a king, things are going to get spicy. When you grow into the world changer God is calling you to be by using your business for mission, you'll be placing yourself on the field, where an opponent is waiting.

Challenges will come.

They won't always be small ones.

They won't always be pleasant and they're not going to come from the natural realm no matter how much they look like they are. They're going to come in the same way a football team walks onto the field knowing the opponent's defensive team is going to come at them. That's the game, and you can't play it without both sides. If you did, the win would be hollow.

The overriding message of Scripture is that there is an Enemy, he hates God, and by extension he hates God's children (you and me). He's actively working to thwart whatever God wants to do because that's the kind of bully he is.

Don't shy away from the challenge.

You were made for this.

You were made for now.

You've got this, because God's got you.

He knew exactly when He'd place you here, what He'd need you to do, and He put everything you need in your heart and mind. The journey is simply unlocking those gifts, growing into those gifts, and starting to believe that it's possible.

Be bold, confident, strong, full of faith and excitement knowing that you're part of a global team doing incredible things with Jesus as your quarterback. He needs you; He wants you, and most importantly He's called you and your entrepreneurial heart for this very purpose.

Spiritual warfare and Mr. Bully are just part of playing that game.

Burning voodoo dolls have never been found on my front lawn. Neither have witch doctors. I don't look for the crazy in life, but I do want my eyes to be open like Elisha's servant so I can see what's out there, what's happening, and respond appropriately. The undercurrent and subtle coincidences that combine to negatively impact our lives aren't there by chance. When people bring disunity into your family, or disharmony into your team, recognize it and rise up in faith to deal with it.

When people work against you or don't work for you, keep looking *through* them to see who's behind it all, and take strength from Scripture that God has you covered, if you stay on His plan.

CHAPTER 11
WHEN GOD LEADS

I started this year much like the others, with good intentions and a few "resolutions" I felt comfortable I could hit. I failed pretty hard on the no chocolate thing (I'm starting a local chapter of "Chocoholics Anonymous," feel free to join me, the weekly entry fee is a box of Cadbury's).

I'm still on track to read one book each week though, and no, they're not all twenty-page pamphlets. If a book goes over two hundred pages though, can I count it as two?

As January was rolling through, something happened that caught me by surprise. I haven't decided if I really like surprises yet, because on the one hand they're awesome. Getting something or seeing something happen you weren't expecting can be seriously fun.

On the other hand, not all surprises are good ones.

You know what I mean.

Don't judge.

. . .

If I'd known ahead of time that I was getting more chocolate for Father's Day I could have said no. Because it was a surprise, I *had* to eat it. The fact it was Cadbury's Fruit and Nut just made it even more irresistible. Turning it down would have been like rejecting an invitation for tea from the Queen.

Now I'm not one of those folks who claims to hear God speaking a whole lot. Sometimes I don't hear anyone speak because my brain is in its own bubble. Other times, though, I get a sense that God is nudging me and I spend the next few days or weeks trying to figure out if it was really Him or not.

Once, I was worshipping in a local church on a Sunday morning and I had one of these moments. A thought dropped into my mind about sending a few thousand dollars across the world to some friends.

Seemed strange for sure, but we could handle it, so Linda and I figured, "What the heck, God or not it sounds like a fun thing to do."

Later we found out the money we sent helped pay for an unexpected funeral for one of their kids.

I wrestled with that.

Why nudge me to send money when He could have simply kept them alive?

This year I had that same feeling.

It was as though my prayers to hear His voice were finally working.

I blocked out the noise in my mind as much as I could, and the message still seemed to be the same, so I'm pretty sure it was Him.

He spoke about generosity.

Which is strange because I think I'm a pretty generous person. Or at least I did until I heard the number He was talking about. Then I changed into a crazed, selfish, spoiled little child wanting to hold on to all nine hundred of his teddy bears because sharing *one* just wouldn't be fair. I need them *all* for Pete's sake.

After wrestling with the number for a few days, it was time to sit Linda down and chat about my epiphany for the year. We've been married for a while so she knows how to read me when I say something like, "Hey, baby, we should sit down for a minute and chat." She follows my statement with a look that says, Is this a chat about serious stuff or a chat about the kids' dinner? We both know which look on my face says what at that point.

Linda's been pretty awesome over the years. As if being married to an entrepreneur isn't bad enough, she got one who also wanted to change the world for Jesus so it's like a double whammy.

I explained what I thought I was hearing. She nodded. Gave a little smile and said "Okay."

Okay what?

Didn't she get it?

We'd be cleaning out an entire account. And then some.

One with more zeros than we'd ever dreamed of as a young married couple. Worse, we wouldn't even be spending it on us!

She played it cool, and we agreed it would be more fun spending it on Jesus anyway, but then the work began.

What do we do, how do we do it? Who do we donate to, support, and invest into so we can deliver sustainable, lasting impact in the lives of those who benefited? The how isn't as important as the result for me.

It's the OUTCOME that I focus on.

The number was bigger than anything we'd ever done, so I took the challenge seriously and started reading (remember that whole book a week challenge?). Researching, learning, and looking for organizations and people to partner with on projects that align with our hearts (like human trafficking and abandoned children).

What's been absolutely amazing to me is how hard it's been to invest in the kingdom and give money away. Seriously.

That's not an invitation for you to stalk me on social media and tell me all about the amazing project your church is working on.

Haven't you been reading?

I'm responsible for this one.

God spoke to me.

Challenged me.

I have to step up and show I'm a good steward, and that means I have to get involved, be involved, and be comfortable that the things we invest in will deliver the greatest impact possible in helping and changing lives, whether or not someone finds Jesus along the way.

Although I hope they do.

He's awesome.

But He didn't try to convert everyone before helping them, so I don't think I need to either.

Blind giving isn't in my vocabulary because Jesus told a story about servants managing someone else's resources and how that went down upon his return. Speaking of returns, we've already seen that God expects them.

How's your balance looking?

The story about the talents that Jesus told clearly shows He was happy with the folks who took what they had and made more, and He was unhappy with the guy who protected what he had, just keeping it safe. Whatever the talent was isn't a concern for me. The growth expected is what counts.

Which one are you?

Which one am I?

For this to work I only have one mode of operation. We talked about it in the last chapter. Questions. Lots of questions. Most of the time more than twenty-one.

Why do I have so many questions? Because I need to know that they have answers. Lots of answers. If they don't, then I'm not buying.

I'm halfway through the year and I'm failing.

I'm also worried.

I'm worried that I won't hit the goal before the end of the year.

I'm worried there's not enough hours in the day for me to implement some of the ideas I've been having to try to help fix that.

I'm worried because I just don't understand what some of the people I've visited were thinking. They're scratching around for crumbs from anyone who'll give them when God has real resources in the hands of His modern-day kings untapped and sitting idly by.

It's frightening that as a global Church, we continue

viewing the impact of our work and the efficiency of achieving it on a different scale from the real world. It's frightening how many people think just because we can write a check that's bigger than "more," that we should. With little to no meaningful measurables or tracking mechanisms in place.

Asking for more doesn't work for me.

Why would it? I need to know that funds are handled appropriately, with no excess, don't you? If you want to live in a big house and drive a nice car, that's awesome, but I'm not paying for it.

So don't ask me to.

The call is like a triple-tiered system.

First, when we're living paycheck to paycheck, just starting out and growing in life, we can fund and support others doing great things through our giving and donations pretty simply.

As we move into the second tier and hit some meaningful income, we start to think bigger, and look to partner with or work with others, dipping our toe in the mission but not fully committing. It may be because we still think the "professionals" have it under control, it may be because we don't have a fully realized theology of stewardship and kingship. Whatever the reason, it's a stepping-stone into our destiny, and to stay here would be wrong.

Finally, we hit the third tier. Where we recognize that it isn't someone else's job, it's ours. God hasn't called someone else to touch the world in a particular way, He's called us to. He's calling us to commit real resources, not scraps. Time, money, our staff, our everything, so we can bring our expertise, intelligence and giftings to His mission field.

I've learned that God is really chatty, and there's a ton of business owners who are listening to Him speak, every single day. Trying to figure out how we can play the game on the Marketplace field better during our forty, fifty, or sixty hours a week. There's so much opportunity it's crazy. It's bigger than any commercial opportunity you can find. With bigger rewards and an eternal legacy.

Because we're built to lead, we need to lean into it.

We're already leading daily; we just need to grow that leadership into mission and kingdom projects too. This is where the friction comes between Church and king, you can't have two leaders with two different visions. You can only have one.

We're already being led by Jesus.

Every day.

For our business and our home.

The ministry folks need to mimic the priests and prophets, coming alongside our vision to pray, support, and help however they can. When they take the time to get behind us and see what God's up to, they'll start to see how much better this system is. We're not trying to cut anyone out; we're trying to bring them in. But we're leading the charge because we're the kings.

They'll get to know us and learn about our strengths, giftings, and calling. They'll better understand what we face on the field every day of the week, warfare, persecution, and countless other challenges.

They'll start to realize that guilting us for not making a Wednesday night service or a Saturday morning men's breakfast is just plain idiocy. Our time is the most valuable thing we have. Saturday morning might be the *only* morning all week that we're not on the clock and in a hurry. Why would anyone schedule something for us to get to and pull us away from some much-needed rest?

Cray cray.

Beauty sleep literally has sleep in its name.

So, help us stay beautiful.

I came across a group of entrepreneurs that were pursuing God in a serious way, looking for guidance through a prophetic session.

There were no pagan gods involved.

Or witchcraft.

We're talking about Paul's letter to the Corinthians here, people, and the spiritual gifts he wrote about.

We sought God for answers that we could check and validate against Scripture. Solid words from heaven that could shift things for us in some way, as we work out our faith on a daily basis. Wanting to please Him in the kingly anointing He's given us.

It was awesome, accurate, and refreshing.

But I've only ever found it once, in decades of searching.

We need more of this. But it didn't come through a church or local leadership.

It came through a king.

An entrepreneur.

Helping other entrepreneurs.

Acting like a priest.

My coworking business exists entirely because it was God's idea.

No, seriously.

He spoke in exactly the same kind of way over a decade ago. I was church planting before I knew better, and He spoke clearly. Multiple times. He spoke about my current business that I run today. While I was church planting with no interest or idea that He had a different plan for me.

I only realized it years later. Here's how it went down.

We were planting and I was being a rock star pastor. I had the cool jeans, the shirts that twenty-somethings wear, and I was rockin' them in my thirties. We met in a dance studio that was awesome. Black ceilings, 2700k, soft white downlights on dimmer switches so we could get the atmosphere just like heaven, because we all know they turn the lights down up there when Jesus hits the stage.

It was neat, and it worked great for us. The owners were so awesome they let us store our gear there through the week (if you've never been part of a new church startup meeting in a borrowed building and packing up gear every week you have missed out on life, people).

I even did the American church thing and slapped a big vinyl banner on the side of the feeder road (did I mention we fronted right onto the freeway) with my picture on it.

Me and Linda.

Bigger than life size.

In one of those cool Ed Hardy shirts.

We'd done everything we could think of, so we waited for the lines to start growing like a Chick-fil-A at lunchtime.

They didn't show up quite like that. But God did.

• • •

Our covering pastors visited one day, and they live out what I'm writing about here. They recognized God's business anointing on me almost twenty years earlier when I was youth pastor at their church in the great metropolis of Lake Jackson, Texas. At the time, neither of us really understood what that meant.

Hence the twenty-year gap.

As they prayed with us in the building, they started to speak words from heaven straight into our lives.

"God has a building for us," they said.

"An incredible building that looks like a government building. With lots of rooms or compartments in it and there are people everywhere."

Oh, and it was maybe one mile away from where we were currently meeting.

If you're starting a church and someone says something like that to you, prefacing it with anything that sounds like "God wants you to know" then holy moly, it's like winning the lottery. At least I think it is because I've never won.

But I had a client who won once.

$291 million.

Anyway, we thought this was it.

Manna from heaven was on the way.

America needed another megachurch, and we were going to bring it. We were pumped. The room was electric like the front row of a Michael Jackson concert waiting for the moonwalk and before nobody liked him anymore.

. . .

As we processed the information, I couldn't help but hang on the thought of it being a government building. Surely that had to be pretty mega, right?

The future didn't work out quite the way we planned. I'm not talking "dead if I don't get eight million dollars wrong" like the preacher I mentioned earlier in this book, but different.

My budding church startup wound up with my good buddy Luke, who took over the reins while I recovered from an auto accident. While recovering and working to keep paying the bills like a want-to-be actor waiting tables in LA, a different idea came to mind.

It was 2013 and working from home wasn't cool back then.

It also wasn't working.

For me.

Between homeschooled kids and a noisy wife (just kidding, kind of), I needed quiet. So, I went looking for it, but couldn't find it, at a price point I could afford, in a place I'd actually want to work in.

I figured I could build something. Something awesome. And others would come. Just like Kevin Costner.

So I did.

And they did.

It's a coworking business called WorkLodge. You can check it out online but if you do, be a love and leave us a five-star review. I'll put in a good word for you with Jesus when I hang with Him next. I pinky promise.

Two years after opening our first location, we opened our second. It was 2017. Around five years after that message from heaven about a building with lots of rooms or compartments.

It just so happens that number two is in the same town as that old dance studio we did church in all those years earlier. The actual building didn't exist back then, as it was constructed in 2015 and opened in 2016, around three years *after* that message from heaven.

To be clear, it didn't exist when my pastor spoke those words.

We're on the top floor with almost a hundred offices (that kind of look like compartments or rooms) and there are people everywhere!

I finally started to grasp this concept of entrepreneurship as a vehicle for mission. Of how God wants to fuse business with mission to deliver a larger scale of impact. Because He spoke, and the picture became clear after stepping out in faith, I began to realize that there was more to His story than the two-dimensional view of ministry I'd believed my whole life.

But that's not the whole story.

It's now late 2021, and it's been four years since we opened. A new tenant is moving in after a year of construction. They're the largest tenant in the entire building, taking more square footage than anyone else including us, and we have our name on the building!

What's their name?

The Department of Homeland Security.

A government agency.

Coincidence?

Mind blown.

. . .

This had God's fingerprints all over it and we knew it, and when I look out the windows on the west side can you guess what I look at across the street?

A cute little dance studio from that old church plant.

Less than a mile away.

CHAPTER 12
ELASTIC GENEROSITY

Linda and I had been house hunting for around three years when in one twenty-four-hour period, we both separately came across the same home, and realized it checked almost all the boxes we had (there's no pool which checked my box but didn't check hers, so I guess God loves me more…).

She saw it on Friday afternoon, and I found it Friday night, half asleep while killing time on my iPad for no specific reason other than I didn't want to go to sleep.

I have this theory that if I stay up later, then my day doesn't end as quickly, so it feels as though I got more out of the day. I think it's flawless logic no matter what time I wake up so let's just leave it there.

It's like turning up the volume to eleven.

It *has* to be louder than ten, right?

We went to view the home twelve hours later and that was that. We broke the Guinness world record for our realtor from phone call (10 a.m.) to viewing (2 p.m.) to agreeing the deal (10 p.m.) and closing everything out a couple weeks later.

She only came out one time to show us anything.

I'm glad she was awesome.

Because it was easy money.

When the day came to close, I went to the bank to pick up a cashier's check because for some reason, they still want you to hand over real money at the title company when you sign the documents.

Who knew?

I walked into the bank having called ahead of time to make sure there wouldn't be any issues, and was greeted by the front desk cashier, which was a little weird. He knew my name before I'd even spoken and I'm not *that* famous. Now I'm wondering whether my bank profile says, "Handsome bald guy who would look like Ross from *Friends* if he had hair."

I explained I was there to pick up my check, we confirmed the amount, and he handed it over.

He asked if we were moving to which I replied, "I sure am."

The small talk was nice.

He'd clearly been trained on it.

What he didn't ask was why we needed such a large amount of money. I guess it was obvious, even though for a split second it would have been cool to say, "I'm headed to Vegas and putting it all on red."

He didn't ask me if I thought I was being wise.

He didn't ask if I was getting a good deal.

He didn't wrestle internally as he made out the check, sweating buckets as he wrote the words.

He didn't do anything strange at all. He simply handed me the check, exchanged goodbyes, and carried on with whatever he was doing.

Do you know why he didn't do those things?

Wait for it…

Because it wasn't his money.

I was *withdrawing* what was already mine.

I'd *lent* it to the bank in a transactional way. We both understood I could come back at any time and ask for it back but until then, they were free to use it however they liked. We might say they were stewarding what I'd lent them for the good of their shareholders, but they and I always held a clear understanding that the money was never theirs, it was always mine. Even while they held it for me.

As Christian entrepreneurs and business owners we need to own this concept in our lives also, because our businesses are the same.

They're not ours.

We're taking care of them for a while on behalf of the true owner. And it's super important we grasp this concept.

It's not yours.

It's not mine.

None of it.

God gives us life, breath, health, and creativity, to use as we think best, but ideally to use in line with His purpose and plan for our life. If you're a business owner or entrepreneur with a heart for Jesus, I say this in love.

· · ·

It means that when you make decisions, you can't make them based on logical data sets alone. You need to make them through the lens of a spiritual and eternal data set too.

You can't make decisions based on only what's best for you. You need to consider what's best for Jesus also.

Remember the whole "what you did for the least of these you did it as though it was me" story a couple chapters ago?

Want to expand your business?

Great.

What does God think about it?

Not hearing from Him?

Then figure out how to *before* taking another step.

Because it's His. Not yours.

You and I are the bank teller, my friend. We never get to look at the vault thinking, "Woohoo, time to hit the casino and party." I don't know why I keep going to Vegas and casinos. I promise I don't have a gambling problem.

We're to look at the vault and *always* understand that everything inside it belongs to someone else, we're simply taking care of it until the true owner comes calling.

Jesus. A.k.a. God.

Now hold that thought for a minute and we'll come back to it.

I read about a TV evangelist years ago, whose wife was confused about the show. She asked him how often they talked about salvation, in other words, how clearly they explained to people watching or listening that their lives could be transformed if they chose to follow Jesus. He wasn't sure how often they did, but he was sure it must be "pretty often."

She then asked how often they tell people about the importance of giving, of tithing to the ministry. "Oh, every week," was his reply.

Classy.

Did you know the word tithe isn't in the New Testament? I think it's because Paul hated it just as much as I do. It's like a swear word so from now on, we'll treat it like an F-bomb and call it the T-bomb instead because bombs aren't good. They destroy things.

And so does this word.

My bet is the New Testament authors had seen what legalism had done to people and knew there was a better way. They'd witnessed first-hand how selfish and greedy people are, knowing that we inevitably try and find any way possible to keep hold of as much of anything as possible.

Just look at the buffet line next time you're at Golden Corral.

If I'm rocking your world right now stay with me because when we get hung up on legalism, we run into problems real fast. When people talk about the T-bomb it seems to raise a lot of questions.

1. Gross or net pay?
2. Should a business T-bomb or just the folks who earn a salary from it?
3. If a business should, and it's from the net because that's what we actually get, then net of what? If you're a business owner, is it net of COGS (cost of goods sold)? Any business owner worth his salt

knows how easy it is to maneuver that number. If
your $150,000 Tesla is on the books as part of your
costs of doing business and you're giving off the net,
you're already stealing from God.

We're only a couple questions in and we're already unstuck.

We've already found loopholes and gray areas to manipulate the numbers down, so we give less, keep more, and sleep like a baby at night as though we did God a favor by hitting the goal.

Ten percent isn't the goal.

It never was.

I had a friend a few years back who endured what I can only assume to be a painful divorce (I met him much later so I didn't get to live through it with him). He had young children and was a single dad, making an okay living but covering everything by himself. We talked about giving once. God had blessed him tremendously since those earlier days and he made a comment that rocked my legalistic world.

When he paid his rent, vehicle costs, food bill, and finally bought clothes for the kids for school, he didn't have 10 percent left.

I didn't pry, but I don't think he even had 0.1 percent left.

As I remembered that story, I thought about a book I recently read that, without any hesitation or gentleness, laid out a theory of legalistic giving that still amazes me today. The author effectively said that because my buddy didn't write his tithe check first AND make sure it was paid before any other money went out, he might as well have not bothered giving anything because *he'd already failed to honor God's law in how to tithe.*

I genuinely felt a little throw up in my mouth when I read it.

Even now, I want to jump in my truck, drive down to his house, and lay my sweet Jesus-loving hands all over him.

How can anyone seriously think God isn't pleased with our generosity because it wasn't literally the first dollar to leave our account?

The New Testament sure doesn't say that.

How can anyone think my buddy giving out of what he hasn't got (0.1 percent) is somehow offensive to God compared to a billionaire giving God a hundred million dollars?

One of them has nothing left, the other has nine hundred million somethings.

It might just be me, but I'm thinking the billionaire could have given two hundred million and lived on the eight hundred million left.

Tough, I know, but doable.

Jesus made a point to address this when He was in the temple one day hanging with His posse, people-watching.

*"Jesus was in the temple, observing all the wealthy wanting to be noticed as they came with their offerings. He noticed a very poor widow dropping **two small copper coins** in the offering box. 'Listen to me,' he said. 'This poor widow has given a larger offering than any of the wealthy. **For the rich only gave out of their surplus, but she sacrificed out of her poverty and gave to God all that she had to live on'"** (Luke 21:1–4).*

It's not about a percentage.

It's not about an amount.

It's about proportionality.

It's about elasticity.

It's about understanding that if we aren't returning enough of what is already God's back to God that it makes us sweat, then we aren't walking in faith and we aren't trusting Him. But what makes me sweat can be very different than what makes you sweat.

It's relative.

Subjective.

And not buttoned up with a bow on top.

God is well able to catch our attention sooner or later. Not because He's punishing us or being a bully, but because He loves us and wants us to experience the blessing that comes out of a faith walk grounded in proportional, extravagant generosity.

He's also well within His rights to do that because it's all His anyway. But like anyone in love, He doesn't play the "rights" card.

Paul brings more clarity on this in his letter to the Corinthians.

*"Remember this: Whoever sows sparingly will also reap sparingly, and whoever sows generously will also reap generously. Each of you should give **what you have decided in your heart** to give, **not reluctantly or under compulsion**, for God loves a cheerful giver. And God is able to bless you abundantly, so that in all things at all*

times, having all that you need, you will abound in every good work.
As it is written:
'They have freely scattered their gifts to the poor; their righteousness
endures forever.'
Now he who supplies seed to the sower and bread for food will also
supply and increase your store of seed and will enlarge the harvest of
*your righteousness. You will be enriched in every way **so that you***
***can be generous on every occasion**, and through us your generosity*
will result in thanksgiving to God" (2 Corinthians 9:6–11).

According to Paul, our generosity is a subjective thing.

It's between God and us.

It's not based on a rule or a fee.

Phrases like "decided in your heart to give" and "you'll be enriched in every way so you can be generous" don't sound anything like "pay the tax and the rest is yours."

They don't sound like that because they don't mean that.

On purpose.

The practical reality of why churches focus so heavily on the T-bomb is because humans are selfish, greedy by nature, and make bad decisions.

Not just church folk. I'm talking about the leaders too!

They build huge buildings by borrowing money and then try to figure out how to pay for them. They build teams of professionals who all need a paycheck instead of pushing them to the Marketplace, to serve like Jesus, where they'd be getting a paycheck AND finding themselves in a more impactful place for mission.

Don't think you're off the hook.

I'm not either.

We're selfish and greedy too. We want a number to aim for. We don't want to make the decision because deep down we know we'll make the wrong one.

Have you ever noticed how cheap people are when being asked to give something away but generous when someone else is trying to give something to them?

We like targets, and 10 percent is easy for us to process.

"As much as He wants" is a little harder to quantify.

If a preacher told you "God owns it all and today, He wants it all back" you'd probably run for the door just as fast as you can. I doubt you'd head back.

But He does.

And I'm not writing for butts in pews.

I have no vested interest in taking your money.

I don't want it.

I don't need it and frankly, if you give it to me, I'm just going to give it away.

That might be okay with you but it's still wrong. The whole point of this book is that it's wrong.

God didn't bless you so you can give it to me to handle for you. He blessed you because He wants YOU to handle it. Don't rob yourself of the growth and work God wants to perform in *your* life, as He builds *your* story, through *your* journey of generosity.

It's the journey that's so critical for us entrepreneurs.

I'm not writing for everyone, and I know it. I'm writing to those who recognize our system is flawed. Who understand that 10 percent can't change the world. But it's world change that's needed. Nothing less.

Just look around.

I'm writing to kings of their own kingdoms. Leaders, business owners, entrepreneurs, and others whom God has blessed in a financial way.

That blessing brings with it an adventure. That doesn't mean you should buy a bigger boat, but it does mean God's blessing came with strings attached. He can do that, you know, because He's God.

It comes with an obligation to fund and further His kingdom, using *every available resource* He's given to you, not just one. It's not just implied, it's automatic. The Great Commission is for us to take God's kingdom to the world and show them Jesus. Your job and mine is to figure that out however we can, using our wisdom and knowledge to do it better, faster, bigger.

There's no negotiation which means we aren't keeping 90 percent. We aren't even keeping 80 percent.

Paul wrote that earlier passage to the Corinthian people because he was an entrepreneur. It's written from a business owners' perspective, in business language.

The person sowing and reaping is a farmer, an entrepreneur.

Sowing and reaping is a business activity for the farmer.

He's also the owner of the field.

He's the one who buys the seed and plants it.

He expects a return on his investment.

He's the one who gathers it, but don't miss this...

He's the one who gives generously from what he reaps.

Not from the initial seed he had.

There're so many layers to this I don't have space to dig into them all but there's two things we can't miss:

First, there's an expectation of growing what God gives us as entrepreneurs, just like Jesus explained in His story of the talents.

Second, it does no one any good if the farmer takes from the seed he has and gives it away *before* he plants it.

This is why as entrepreneurs, our generosity and giving doesn't run from week to week or month to month, because we don't live or exist on regular paychecks like most people do. We need to invest, and reinvest to grow our businesses, developing long-term stability.

That's how you grow a business.

It's precisely because of this that it's prudent and necessary for us to view our giving over months and years vs. days and weeks. We're not short-term thinkers so don't let anyone tell you otherwise.

I don't care whether I give a thousand dollars to kingdom work this week or next month, and I don't think God sweats it too much either. He can get my attention quickly if He needs to. Remember, He's the one who walked everywhere for three years. He didn't even run to save time, let alone ride a horse.

Think about that.

We never read of Him running.

Not even speed walking.

He knows that before the end of the year I sit down and analyze the numbers, making sure I close out where I want to be, where I've decided ahead of time, without compulsion or persuasion from anyone or anything.

If God needs me to give more, I need to hear His voice at the start of the year, when I'm planning and setting goals. Not at the end of the year because of someone's slick, smooth talking.

Remember, His blessing and mantra of giving us our entrepreneurial hearts in the first place wasn't for our benefit, it was for His. Sure, we get to enjoy a little of it, but if we're enjoying more of it than God's getting, maybe the balance is wrong?

When I started my current business, I didn't take one dollar out of it for myself until I was well into the second year.

When I did, my first paycheck was a thousand dollars.

For the month.

I also didn't give God much of anything during that time. But the business was making money.

The logic of some people says that I'd be cursed for stealing from God.

But I wasn't and I'm not.

Why?

I think there's 4 key reasons:

1. Although I wasn't giving to Him, I wasn't taking it for me either.
2. Although there was gain or profit, it was being reinvested entirely to build a stronger business that would deliver a 10x return tomorrow instead of a 1x return today. I was planting my seeds.

3. I'd intentionally and purposefully laid out our plans to our customers and friends, making it clear for everyone to see how the for-profit business existed to fund the nonprofit entity. So, we began working through the nonprofit to find programs we could align with and support.
4. I sacrificed.

Let's take a time out here and look at that last point for a second because practically, you probably have some questions. I'm sure not here to tell you how to live your life but if you're curious, here's what sacrifice looked like for us.

1. It meant understanding and living out the principle of spending less than you bring in for years before we took the leap. Without that foundation and those savings, we couldn't have made it work.
2. It meant staying in a less expensive home than we could afford despite wanting to move, because Linda and I always figured God would eventually come knocking with a big task to do and we didn't want to be caught short.
3. It meant walking away from a well-paying job and leaping out in ridiculous faith. With no background or experience in commercial real estate and no support or funding other than our savings (and the kids' piggy banks), we signed a ten-year lease worth millions of dollars on nothing more than a hunch

    that God was in this, and it was His idea in the first
    place.

4. It meant driving a reasonably priced vehicle instead of a nice one.
5. 5It meant very few dinners out, activities out, and turning down a whole lot of fun.
6. It meant no vacations, simple holidays and one monthly luxury subscription. Netflix. The bottom tier. I just upgraded to 4k. Yesterday. Other than that, only essential bills were allowed.

Your story could be different, and your future may look entirely different to my past. But the key for me was knowing I needed to make it at least a year without money coming in (personally), to help build a cushion into year two for the business.

So we did.

And that included giving.

Maybe that cost Jesus ten thousand dollars.

I don't know for sure.

What I do know is that the last check we wrote for Jesus added a zero to hit a hundred thousand dollars. A 10x improvement.

This year we're adding another zero.

Then we'll be aiming for another as soon as we can because we need to be sure He always comes out ahead.

Way ahead.

And continues to stay there.

I call it the law of Elastic Generosity and it's built around a four-tiered system that helps us understand how to give. We'll go deeper into it in the next chapter.

In my example from the experiment we've been living through with WorkLodge, by sowing profits back into the business early on, we were able to reap a stronger harvest that has enabled us to give exponentially more. Through a combination of partnerships, donations, and our own profits, we should finish this year having sowed the equivalent of seven million dollars into impact initiatives and projects that directly benefit the people they serve through our nonprofit, Gabriel.

To get a little granular, Linda and I operate from a mindset that Jesus should make more from the business than we do.

Every year.

And that's how it should be.

Not because of some legalistic requirement.

Not because of some crazy rule.

Because we love Him, and understand it was never ours in the first place. I'm just excited that I get paid anything, to do something, that changes everything. I don't mean by taking the easy way out and just giving it to someone else to handle. I mean by taking the tough way out and moving up the tiers of generosity we're going to look at next.

When you think about giving, about generosity, or about the T-bomb, I want to give you some freedom and permission to stop listening to what others say and start listening to your heart. Ask God to nudge you. Consider what Paul wrote about how we give, not under compulsion or because we must. Think about your business, about how much comes in and how you choose to let it go out, and start making some changes.

Make sure God wins big.

Make sure you win small.

Don't trust someone else to handle it.

You handle it.

Start to see what you've been trusted with as exactly that, something you've been trusted with that isn't yours. Recognize that your business brings other resources that can help the mission also. Your team, your assets, your relationships, and your friends. Above it all, enjoy the freedom of thinking strategically, over months and years, to deliver the biggest impact for Jesus you can possibly bring. That's when you'll start to have the real fun. Helping others and changing lives.

CHAPTER 13
BOMBS AWAY

I love Jesus.

I want to make sure you know that because I'm going to challenge the T-bomb in more detail in this chapter. It's a pointless and meaningless concept that is often used to manipulate, guilt, shame, and control people.

Calm down.

I really do love Jesus.

Have you ever heard someone talk about giving? Dropping the T-bomb all over Sunday morning like it's gummy bears being thrown into the hands of school kids?

These legalistic mini sermons aren't helpful.

You start to feel guilt or shame if you think you're not doing it right. The way *they* say it should be done, but the teaching misses a far bigger perspective the Bible teaches about stewardship.

Every single business I've started meant going without a

salary for a certain amount of time. It's okay, I knew that was part of the deal when I started them and it's part of the trade. You can't win big if you don't bet big and so my "bet" was living cheap and going without, in the hope that one day I wouldn't have to unless I chose to.

It was a good bet.

Now I don't have to.

I used to hear preachers drop the T-bomb and feel the guilt trying to wrap itself around me. I started to second-guess myself.

I wondered if I should be pulling more money out so I could be a "good Christian" and check the box. But just because the business was making money, I wasn't. So how was I supposed to give while reinvesting everything into growing something, building something that would ultimately enable me to give exponentially more?

I had everything riding on each one of those ventures.

This is the problem with teaching everyone that God has the same expectations from us all. He doesn't because He knows some of us are more capable than others.

He made us that way!

It's the same with our kids.

If one of them is gifted in sports, we push them harder because we know they're capable. If another is gifted in academics and can't throw a ball more than twenty feet, we don't expect the same from them.

We expect something different.

I don't think I should be treated today as the same Mike

who made seven dollars an hour flipping burgers at McDonald's all those years ago.

I'm not the same now as burger flipper Mike then.

My self-discipline isn't the same.

My financial position isn't the same.

My responsibilities and liabilities aren't the same.

There's very little that *is* the same between us outside of our charming good looks, but the Church continues to miss that. It expects me to behave the same way now as I did then, because of its failure to recognize the king anointing that comes with entrepreneurship.

Burger-flipping Mike had rent of less than five hundred dollars each month.

Today Mike has rent of six figures each month.

Burger-flipping Mike had zero mini-mes who depended on him. Today Mike has a whole team of staff who depend on him.

As well as vendors. Partners. And family.

I'm not trying to belittle anyone, but let's recognize that entrepreneurs, business owners, and business leaders are living with, dealing with, and operating in an incredibly different world to the average person.

Expecting little league players to play by the same rules as the big leagues is crazy. It's also unbiblical.

Then there's the technicality of the T-bomb.

We don't have anything to give.

I'm not joking.

We don't have anything to T-bomb because we don't have anything. Period. None of it is ours.

Still not joking.

Remember the banker story? The money was mine all along and the cashier knew it. The parable of the bags of gold is the same. The master returned and asked for an accounting of *his* gold. The stewards might have been trusted with it, but that trust was temporary.

It was never theirs.

Nor was the increase.

It was all his.

Have you ever thought about it?

I hadn't for the longest time. Until one day I did. Then I sat down and took a deep breath. To be fair, it was more like hyperventilating with a brown paper bag on a plane when the pilot says we're "experiencing turbulence" while passengers bounce around as though they're riding Goliath at six flags without a seat belt, blindfolded, and backward.

In both situations, life would never be the same moving forward.

Don't sweat.

Let's get through this together. But first, repeat after me three times before clicking the heels of your ruby-red slippers.

None of it is mine. It's all His.

None of it is mine. It's all His.

None of it is mine. It's all His.

If you remember nothing else from this book, remember that statement, because I can't communicate it strongly enough. It breaks the curse of the T-bomb and proves how irrelevant, outdated, and harmful it is to God's kingdom.

God doesn't want your T-bomb.

He doesn't want *your* anything.

He wants *His* everything.

To do with what He purposed to do.

The illusion that God blesses us so we can live the high life is a lie. From you know who. We talked about him earlier.

Jesus didn't die so you can drive a Rolls-Royce. As though a Bentley isn't good enough. He didn't die so you can buy a bigger house (although both of those may be okay, in the right circumstance).

Jesus came to earth to save people.

He's so serious about it He literally sacrificed His life to do it.

Why could we possibly think He'd do all that for a Rolex?

When God speaks or nudges about money, He's not *asking* me to *give.* He's letting me know He's ready to make a withdrawal of *His* resources from the bank of Mike. He's also rarely asking successful entrepreneurs for that withdrawal to be handed to someone else (like a non-profit or ministry organization). He's given you success, wisdom, intelligence and a team of people because He thinks you can use them to impact your community. The withdrawal isn't just for money, He wants to withdraw from your time bank, your intellect bank and your skill set bank.

That withdrawal is His to make, and just like that teller, my only option is to say, "Yes, sir, let me get that for you."

Start there.

Stay there.

Because that's where freedom reigns.

There's another story Jesus told that's helpful. He was in

full, parable-telling flow when He dropped this little two-line nugget:

"God's kingdom is like a jewel merchant on the hunt for exquisite pearls. Finding one that is flawless, he immediately sells everything and buys it" (Matthew 13:45–46).

It reminds me of a story I read about someone else who found what he thought was a great pearl. His name was Rene.

He was a pop singer in Canada when, in 1972, he decided managing artists might be better than being one. I guess it wasn't an easy ride because by 1981, he was ready to quit and go to law school. Around the same time a twelve-year-old girl wrote her first song with her mom and brother. They thought it was pretty good, so with a makeshift recording, her brother sent Rene the tape to listen to after seeing his name on the back of another album.

When Rene listened to the tape, he was moved to tears. Literally. So he reached out and began helping them. He set up tours, got them gigs, and a few years later mortgaged his home to produce her first album.

Let that sink in for a second.

He mortgaged his home.

To pay for her *first* album.

Not second.

First.

In 1988 she won the Eurovision Song Contest.

She's since won a ton of other awards and Grammys,

becoming the only artist since Michael Jackson to sell ten million albums in Europe.

She's sold over 220 million albums worldwide and is now worth over eight hundred million dollars.

Her name is Celine Dion.

Oh, and she married Rene in 1994. Seriously. The guy who heard her voice when she was twelve years old and cried.

Rene found his pearl, and no matter the cost was willing to spend it.

Should we be any different for Jesus?

Some people read that verse by Jesus and see how God gave up everything to come buy us, through the cross. Others read it and see it as an allegory of us, how we found an exquisite pearl in Jesus and should be willing to sell everything to "buy" Him.

I'll tell you what I tell Linda regularly, but especially when we're at an Indian restaurant trying to decide between curries.

"Why does it have to be either-or, why can't it be both?"

If God paid the ultimate price for you and me, then why are we worried about how much we can keep and not give back to Him?

It's a joy, a privilege, and an honor to think that He's willing to trust us with *anything* that's His, even if it's not as much as someone else has. I may be a two-talent guy. If I am, then that's how He made me so it's all good. I don't have to worry about handling five or ten talents.

If we really love Him, we won't have an issue being generous toward Him. So why do we have such a hard time letting go of what's not ours?

It's the relativity that's key here.

Because the Bible clearly shows that God is good about taking care of the folks who work for Him. I hear King Solomon did okay. Some people still think he's the richest guy to have ever lived.

Ever.

We talked about this. Estimates range in the $2,000,000,000,000. That's a whole lot of zeros.

Solomon realized it wasn't his. But the *role* God placed him in (as king) required he live a certain way and carry himself appropriately. You may be the same. I may be too. So how do we figure out what's appropriate or not for our lifestyle vs. God's withdrawals?

First, we need to constantly assess how much we're giving back vs. how much we're keeping. Let's be real, folks, those fringe benefits the business covers for you are part of your payment. The vehicle, insurance, cell phone, etc. We don't look to the IRS for guidance, we need to let common sense prevail.

If the business is paying for something you personally enjoy and benefit from, it's a payment of some sort. Don't kid yourself otherwise because it means you didn't have to go spend your own money.

Let's look at a few possible ways we can think about giving back what's already His:

Let's say you're running a ten-million-dollar business with a 20 percent net profit. Net, after everything it costs to run the business, buy your goods, pay down debt, etc. In other words, you're walking away with around $2 million dollars.

The way I've seen most people approach this based on mainstream teaching looks something like this:

$2 million profit minus taxes (approx. $650,000) and a few other miscellaneous things leaves around $1.3 million.

God gets His T-bomb and should thank us while we're at it because we just gave Him $130,000.

We're left with around $1.17 million to do whatever we want with.

New Tesla? No problem.

New home? Sure, we can afford it.

Another way to do this if you want to hang on to that T-bomb just as long as you can, would look more like this:

$10 million revenue = $1 million in giving. I know you've got expenses, so manage them. Do better instead of stealing from Jesus. It's not cool.

That leaves $1 million in profit, or $660,000 after taxes.

Instead of taking home $1.17 m we got half that amount, or $660,000.

But instead of Jesus getting $130,000, we invested $1 million (almost 10x) into the kingdom, storing up our treasure in heaven.

Like Jesus told us to.

"But Mike," I hear you say, "you just told us the T-bomb was evil."

How right you are.

My final suggestion and what I think is the most biblical way to approach things looks more like this:

$2 million in profit = $2 million that's all His.

If you want to be a little amazing, you keep 49 percent and give away 51 percent. So, you keep $980,000 and spend $1.02 million on Jesus.

You.

You spend it.

Not someone else. He trusted you to do something amazing with it!

This is what I'd call my minimum standard. God gets more than I keep, and it's a perfect starting point (remember this is net, so if you need to reinvest for growth, then do that first, but He still receives more than you and me).

The key here isn't to be legalistic or rigid, but to prayerfully set your systems in place *ahead* of time. When the numbers aren't in front of you and don't make you sweat. Remember, Paul said we should base our giving on what we've decided in our hearts, and not under compulsion. That means deciding, and the best decisions happen ahead of time.

When you're not in a hurry.

When you have great data to analyze.

It's easy when the numbers are small. It's harder when they're big.

It's easy to give when you can afford it.

But that's not what we're called to.

The more we have by definition, the more we have to give, just to stay in a place of walking by faith.

The second key is to remember why there's a margin between the two suggestions. It's because giving for us is a sliding scale.

A scale that's relative to your revenue and profitability.

Elastic Generosity.

Let me explain.

For smaller companies in the sub $10 million range, it's

going to be harder to give away as much because there's a point of diminishing returns. If you're the CEO of a $10 million business, you probably can't live on $200,000/year. There's a standard below which you shouldn't go otherwise you'll lessen the respect you receive, and the story you tell of God's goodness and provision in your life won't add up.

It's also less than the average salary of a CEO for a business that size, and I believe we should at least be taking care of ourselves at an average level. We can still give more personally if we want to.

When you reach different levels of revenue, you'll find your circles of friends and influence changing. It happens, so it's important we don't try to keep up with the Joneses. We also don't want to look like we're living by our threads.

As revenues increase it becomes easier to give more.

If you're running a billion-dollar business and walk away with a $200 million net profit, working the 49/51 split isn't even enough.

That's a great starting point for a smaller business in the seven to eight figure profitability range, but now you've hit the big leagues. In this ballpark you should be thinking close to the 90/10 range because you don't need $98 million to live in one year.

$96 million is plenty.

So is $56 million.

To be fair, I could probably scratch by on $36 million a year but not a dime less. My shoe collection changes regularly.

Do you see how the inverse scale works? How elastic generosity functions in a practical way?

I hope so, because it's pretty genius and exactly what we'd expect to see in an upside-down kingdom.

If you need more, the answer isn't to *keep* more, it's to grow your business to *generate* more, having faith in His provision. It's way better than putting all your faith in yourself.

We don't play by the same rules as everyone else (although everyone should remove the T-bomb from their vocabulary), because we're playing on a different field. I want to be part of this revolution that's hitting entrepreneurs and how we view their business, our profit, and our responsibilities. Don't you?

I'm not a fan of cheesy preacher quotes but remember: God won't give to you until God can give through you. He always starts small.

To summarize then, the tiers of elasticity look something like this, and we'll use our B.O.O.M. acronym to help:

1. Baseline Generosity.
If you're living paycheck to paycheck (as most Americans are), you may be able to give 5%, 10% or somewhere in between. You're not in a position to meaningfully impact anything or anyone with that amount by itself so you give it to someone else (a church, ministry, non-profit) so they can combine it with other, similar sized amounts which together, collectively enable a larger impact.

2. Opportunistic Generosity.
This is where I'd see folks making low six figures, whether through a business or as an employee. You're making enough that you can be generous, but still enjoy more than you can

give away. This is where you start to think about things differently.

You might dream of a big project, but you're not quite ready to handle it by yourself. You know you want to make a difference, but you're not quite ready to be able to do it on your own.

3. Obvious Generosity.

You're now making high six figures into the 7 and 8 figure range. By this point, you shouldn't be giving anything to anyone without careful thought and consideration. The numbers are large. 5 to 6 figures at least in generosity which, if you handle wisely, and apply all your resources to it, could make a dent in the lives of many people. This is where your mission begins. If you choose to accept it.

4. Meaningful Generosity.

There might not be many folks at this level, but for those that are, your ability to give Jesus 7, 8 or 9 figures each year means you're absolutely placed to change the world for him. There's going to be people around you telling you to trust them, to give to them as they work to convince you that their next great project is where Jesus is at. I'm not saying it isn't, but I genuinely believe His next great project for you to touch is in your heart, it's in your mind, and it's your mission to make it come alive.

Q&A

You probably have a few questions, so I'll pause for a moment and answer some of them. If you have more, connect with me at www.mikethakur.com and ask whatever you like. I won't tell you where I buy my socks from though, because they're awesome, and I don't want the store to run out.

1. Say I agree with you, Mike. **Are you suggesting I give $5 million to my church as an offering, as God's withdrawal?** NO.

Absolutely not.

That's the absolute worst thing you can do with it. You're a king and a priest in the community of God. He's expecting *you* to lead the way, set the example, and do something with it. We're going to talk about what that looks like using my B.O.O.M. framework soon so stick around.

2. What are the benefits of giving?

First, you're not giving. He's withdrawing.

If you're looking for benefits, you've completely missed it.

3. What principles are involved?

When He says He needs something and you have it, then handle it.

You don't need angels singing in the sky, just train your heart to be sensitive to His spirit.

We talked earlier about the parable of the sheep and the goats and compared it with something James, Jesus' brother, wrote about helping the needy. Both of them said the same thing. If you have the power, capacity, and means to help or take care of something out of love, that benefits His kingdom (and loving people hits the top spot), there's no conversation or debate. God expects you to handle it. It's *why* He put you in a position to be able to.

4. What's in it for me?

Okay, I'll bite.

If you're a legalistic person you'd probably go with something like "not being a thief and stealing from God." I'd rather see it as "fulfilling my destiny, showing God that He was right in trusting me with a little." Another perspective is simply recognizing that we don't need there to be anything in it for us, because we need to be less selfish, recognizing that we're doing okay while someone else isn't. Helping them out can change that so let's help.

Sure, we can talk about growth in faith and trust, learning to follow His lead, etc. but those are principles that are universally applied to our Christian walk, not just the area of generosity.

5. How do we give?

See question 1. We're going to talk about this in a couple of chapters where we'll cover my B.O.O.M. framework, Business Operating On Mission.

For "kings," the expectation is different which is why the system and process needs to be also.

When David had the idea to build a home for God, he set out to plan, design, and create a temple that was worthy of the only supreme being in the universe. Nowhere do we read that David worried about the cost. In fact, no expense could be spared.

Nothing was off limits.

He *wanted* to go big because what else could he do? We're talking about God. The God.

What we see is David using his time, energy and intelligence on the project while bringing in others to help. Stockpiling materials (let's call it saving) and ultimately, having the whole thing ready to go for his son Solomon when he died. David funded it not just from the official royal reserves, but also from his personal accounts as he implored the people to follow his lead.

Estimates put David's *personal* contribution in the hundreds of millions against an overall budget that ran into billions. Can you imagine him sitting there counting out the gold and stopping to announce, "I've hit my 10 percent. No more shall I donate to this project."

He didn't *have* to build anything. He wasn't *asked* to build anything. His heart *demanded* that he build something because he recognized God had given him everything. Maybe that's why God picked him in the first place? Just maybe.

As king, he modeled for kings today the way we should function. Once God puts something on our hearts there's no debate or discussion. If it's in our power, then we go. If it's not, we plan, save, and build up resources until it is.

Sometimes, it seems easier to hold on to our resources rather than spend the time and energy to figure out how to responsibly release them. For now, just remember that you're more valuable to the kingdom as an entrepreneur or business owner than anything else. We'll cover the rest later.

God has placed you here and now for influence.

God positioned you to shine Jesus to your children, your family, your team, your clients, and your partners. He's promoted you so you can be a great steward who generates profit not for your benefit, but for His.

There is no shame in serving God through business.

There is no guilt that you're not in a pulpit.

You're on the field of Marketplace, where you're supposed to be and where the action happens. You're in the *best* place to be. It literally doesn't get any better.

CHAPTER 14
RESPONSIBLE GENEROSITY

Recognizing the need to loosen our grips instead of holding and storing is a great start, it really is. But now what?

What does this really look like in our lives on a practical level? Why do we even need to help others?

To answer those questions, we're going to need to look at something the Bible calls "stewardship," and it's like an onion, because it has so many layers for us to grasp.

You'd think once we've made the decision to be generous and give back to God what's really His anyway, life would get easier. Decisions would be simpler, and we'd all live in a permanent state of bliss.

It's about to get more complicated, and less blissful.

Let me introduce you to my buddy Steve.

Steve grew up in South Africa, and in his teenage years, much like me he felt God tugging him to a life of service. Also like me, he figured that must mean ministry (he's a business guy now), so he pursued it over the next few decades, traveling to countless African nations and preaching about Jesus. He also built a few homes for orphaned children along the way.

One day he was chatting with a local pastor whose church was in dire straits. They needed a new building. They needed a safe, clean environment to meet in and so Steve, feeling the tugging on his heartstrings, agreed to help.

Through his connections and fundraising efforts, he nailed it and raised the funds needed.

Materials were bought and delivered to the site.

Excitement was high.

Months later he was floating on the clouds. As he packed, getting ready to visit the new building for the first time, he felt like one of those America's Got Talent contestants who just saw Simon hit the golden buzzer, while smiling as the gold confetti floated down from above.

When he arrived, everything changed.

The site was dirt.

No foundation.

No structure.

No building.

He was confused. Very confused.

Logic kicked in as he began rationalizing in his mind. "Maybe they built it in a different place?" "Maybe there was a problem with the land?" As the options scrolled through his mind like a ticker tape with stock symbols on it, he went to the pastor's house to get to the bottom of it.

When he arrived, he felt nauseous. Sick in his stomach. Not from the food, but from what he saw as he got out of his vehicle.

The pastor's house was beautiful, brand new in fact. Custom built, and magnificent compared to the other homes around. Steve started to have serious doubts running through his mind about what was going on.

If you're like me, you're having them too right now.

And you'd be right.

The pastor explained that although the materials had been delivered, they'd all been stolen from the construction site before work could commence.

Steve was having none of it. He asked point-blank how the pastor was able to build himself a brand-new home.

"God provided," was the response.

"God provided the exact same bricks, same roofing materials, same everything that had been delivered to the church, but they weren't the same?" asked Steve.

"Yes," the pastor replied.

Lawsuits ensued but were thrown out because without serial numbers or other identifying markings, there was no way to prove that the bricks used on the pastor's home were the same bricks as the ones delivered for the church, even though they looked identical.

The village never got their building. The pastor carried on with life as usual. Steve was devastated.

If you're thinking this kind of thing doesn't happen, it does. If you want to grow into your destiny and walk into your future using God's blessing for impact, it's going to happen to you. Unless you learn from it, develop the skill of *responsible generosity*, and grow up fast.

Anyone can write a check.

We've got to be smarter than that.

Anyone can feel their heart strings being pulled.

We've got to be clearer than that.

We've already established that God will hold us accountable for the returns we deliver to His kingdom. I don't know about you, but the last thing I need is to be worrying that one day I'm going to stand there like the third dude in the story about the talents (let's call him Kevin because he's going to come up a few times in this chapter and "third dude" doesn't roll off the tongue as easily), and God tells me off for being lazy and unproductive.

I'm thinking being one of the first two guys sounds way more appealing.

So I'm shooting for that.

You with me?

Responsible generosity is about so much more than giving a few dollars away. But to truly understand it, we need to evaluate how we view those who should benefit from the work of our hands.

Do you know how poor people outside America see themselves?

Do you know the kinds of words they use to describe their situations or themselves?

I didn't either. It's not a trick question. They use phrases like:

1. Shame
2. Inferiority
3. Depression

4. Guilt
5. Fear
6. Helplessness

If you look at those words, what do you notice?

What do they talk about?

What don't they talk about?

You're probably smarter than I was because I still didn't get it. But they're all emotional phrases. Psychological terms that apply to their state of mind and how they feel.

Do you know how poor people in America describe their situations or how they speak about themselves?

They don't use phrases like that for the most part. They use words and phrases that emphasize a lack of material possessions.

Stuff.

Things.

It's an important distinction because our view of poverty will affect how we tackle the issue.

If we believe it relates to knowledge, then we'll use education as a way to fix it.

If we believe it relates to material resources, then we'll give material resources to fix it.

If we tackle one definition of poverty with the other, "wrong" solution, we're going to blow it. We're going to fail and achieve minimal success.

Worse.

We're going to make the situation worse.

If someone is lacking in education and we give them

"stuff," how does that help them? It's a Band-Aid at best and won't fix the actual problem they have. They need to be educated. If we don't solve that problem, how will they know how to make the best use of the stuff we just gave them?

They won't.

We just made their situation worse.

We became the bad guy, Kevin, of the parable story, except we weren't lazy, and we weren't trying not to do anything. God's issue was with the zero return. And we absolutely nailed it in the example above.

What return did we really achieve here? Was it really a zero?

No. It was worse.

We perpetuated the cycle of poverty.

We kept it going.

Our helping actually hurt. And it's a real thing.

The key isn't to Band-Aid problems or look for the easy, fast solution. We need to look for, focus on, and address the underlying causes. If a doctor only dealt with the symptoms of pain and shortness of breath, without doing anything to help the heart of a patient having a heart attack, then their family will go home devastated later on.

Address the root cause, and the symptoms eventually take care of themselves. It's no different for us.

Our hearts often go out to people in difficult predicaments but giving someone a hundred dollars to pay their light bill does nothing to make sure they won't be in the same situation next month. I'm not saying we don't help. But if we do, we have a mandate to apply the same intelligence, focus, and intentionality that we've given to our businesses to the problem.

Go further.

Go deeper.

Find the root cause and help to fix that.

Maybe they don't make enough money, so help them make more.

Help them job search.

Help them improve their skill set.

Help them grow through education.

There are so many ways they could need to be helped.

Maybe they do make enough money but have a spending problem. Same deal. Help them learn how to budget. Get them signed up to a financial management course like Dave Ramsey's AND walk through it with them.

Hold them accountable. Help them succeed.

I know what you're thinking. My mind-reading skills are pretty impressive, right? You're thinking what I was thinking... That sounds like a lot of work, time, and effort.

And you're right!

So was leaving heaven and coming to live on earth for thirty-three years.

Unlike Jesus though, we were never meant to be the savior of others, because that's His job, and He's not retiring. Or looking to delegate.

We've got to check our hearts and honestly ask ourselves why we want to help. Is it really about him or is it about us? That might sound harsh, but it's pretty common for people to offer help in situations so that *they* receive a sense of relief and satisfaction. We make ourselves feel better because we did something. We pat ourselves on the back as we go buy a couple new Jet Skis. After all, if we helped someone then they must be better off for it.

Right?

Wrong.

Steve Corbett and Brian Fikkert wrote an excellent book on this that you really need to read. *When Helping Hurts* breaks down and examines many of the situations we've all seen as believers. Short-term mission trips that cost more to fly out than if we'd just paid locals to build the wells/homes/churches. Or benevolence funds and neighborhood outreach that create dependency issues without ever addressing the root causes.

Our language for short-term missions is barely enough to conceal the reality that much of the time, these trips are really more like spiritual tourism, which although effective in helping *us* feel as though we're growing closer to God, will not statistically deliver lasting change to the people we're trying to help.

Second is the "savior" complex.

We're riding in to save the day.

We have the answers because we have the money.

We can fix it. They can't.

Wouldn't it be better to just call it a learning experience? An opportunity to learn from the locals in another part of the world. To see the Christian faith lived out in countries where they face daily needs that we would simply never dream of.

I heard about a mission trip to South America. A group rallied together to go and help rebuild the home of one of the local parishioners that had been destroyed. They flew in, spent two weeks rebuilding it as he sat and watched along with his buddies. When they'd finished, they left.

Everyone was high-fiving, pumped and stoked on what they'd accomplished for Jesus. In total, it cost thirty thousand dollars for the team to fly down, stay, and be transported safely on the ground.

Remember those buddies? They were locals with skills. Had they been paid a local wage, they could have built the house for three thousand dollars. Or ten houses for the same thirty thousand dollars spent flying the group down.

Nuts.

Next time you hear someone say they're going on a mission trip to take Jesus to Mexico, maybe gently stop them and ask them when He left.

We don't save the day. He does.

While we're at it, let's be sure to segregate missions into appropriate categories. There's a big difference between global, local, macro, and micro missions.

When Helping Hurts argues (and I think it's right to) that for truly effective missions work to be achieved, we have to address the definition of a biblical framework for poverty. It's pretty helpful and based on an earlier work by Bryant L. Myers. At the end, they conclude that if we're really going to help someone, the only way we can do it is by addressing *all* four foundational relationships that a person was created with:

1. Relationship with God.
2. Relationship with ourselves.

3. Relationship with others.
4. Relationship with the rest of creation.

Why? Because to truly help someone is to help restore them to the fullest expression of their God-created purpose. If we get that right, everything else falls into place. If we don't, nothing we do will truly help or deliver any kind of meaningful, lasting impact.

To be good at this, we've got to make sure we can identify, and value, the giftings God has placed in the hearts of those around us, even if they're not as "successful" as we are (in our eyes). Paul talks about having an honest evaluation of ourselves. Not thinking too highly or lowly is a great place to start. Sure, you might be exceptional at business, but you're still just Joe, or Steve, Vanessa, or Gail. In God's eyes, you are who you are, not what you do. We need to remember that and use the same metrics on ourselves that we use to evaluate others in our circle.

Have you ever noticed that people who travel to poorer, developing nations tend to find Christians whose prayer lives and spiritual lives are like the Hulk compared to ours? I feel like Steve Rogers out of *Captain America* when I pray sometimes. Especially when I prayed on a preaching trip to India.

I don't mean Steve Rogers *after* he was transformed into an invincible fighting machine.

I mean the skinny one.

That everyone laughed at.

The one who couldn't climb a rope.

These folks overseas literally pray for their daily bread,

trusting Jesus to deliver it. On a day-to-day basis. We pray for it doing lip service to a repetitive prayer, knowing full well we have more than enough money in our pockets to buy whatever we want.

Who needs bread?

I like steak.

Whether it's deliberate or unintentional, we project a "we are superior, you are inferior" air toward the people we're trying to help, and because they're desperate to receive that help, they say nothing in return to alert us to the fact.

To bring some clarity as we're thinking through the challenges of trying to be kind and help folks, I've built a simple framework to use if we're looking at a project or opportunity to get involved with that I'm sure will evolve and improve over time. Remember, this is a step on the elastic generosity table but not the final destination. Ultimately, you'll be leading the charge and overseeing your own projects so many of these points won't apply.

1. Clarify how it applies not only to money or capital, but to everything.

Whatever you give (time is more valuable) it needs to be done in a way that GUARANTEES results AND a return.

It's no different than business and the parable of the talents proves this. If you can't see a clear, definite outcome that's a win, returning something better to the kingdom, then walk away no matter how hard your heartstrings pull.

2. Ask the tough questions. Lots of them. Often. Seriously.

If you can't ask questions, or if their answers are noncommittal, nonspecific, or just plain old unhelpful, then walk away no matter how hard your heartstrings pull. This also applies if they don't have answers and always need time to go find them out.

Anyone leading any kind of impactful enterprise should know what they do, how they do it, what they hope to achieve, and how they're going to measure it. If they don't, they aren't the steward you're looking for. They're just someone with a kind heart wanting to do good.

The captain of the *Titanic* had a kind heart too. I still wouldn't get on a boat with him.

3. Make sure you're partnering with others who deserve to be partnered with, are ready to be partnered with, and can handle your partnership.

This is no different than business. You need the right people in the right seats at the right time, all headed in the right direction. Three out of four doesn't work. It's like saying you'd be good with only three engines running on a Boeing 747.

4. Check and validate.

This is something I tell my kids constantly. It works from checking if they took out the trash to the pastor building the church building in Africa. Take baby steps, checking and validating whatever you're being told and whatever milestones have been set along the way (and that means setting milestones).

If someone claims to have built one hundred water wells before, you don't need to see every one of them. But try to see a few and talk to others who have seen more.

Here's a few steps to help:

a. Check out organizations online. Their website. Their affiliations. Their social profiles.

b. Interview everyone you can about them.

c. Use Google—are there comments, reviews, BBB complaints, etc.

d. Look at the Evangelical Council for Financial Accountability website.

e. Visit with them, in person. Interview them, talk to their staff.

f. Give incrementally. Don't send it all at once and don't send large amounts.

5. Make it formal.

Create contracts and documents clearly outlining expectations/milestones etc. Treat any generosity like a business transaction because it is. You're investing something God trusted you with, in the hopes it will deliver impact for His kingdom. Do everything you can to button that up and ensure success. Writing stuff down is a great place to start.

6. Recognize and learn to appreciate you aren't giving away YOUR money/time/resources.

You're giving back to God what's already His and you'll have to answer for it one day. Think of Him like a silent investor if you need to. Who expects results.

7. Build relationships over time.

If you're successful, and especially if you're a million-dollar-profit type of business I guarantee you're going to meet way more people than you can help. They'll find you like Liam Neeson in *Taken*.

They have skills too.

They even buy lists from each other of who the big donors are so they can hit you up for more.

Go slow. If God was in such a hurry to save the world, He could have sent Jesus here for longer, or more than once. He seems to be patient. Let's be patient too, taking our time to get to know people. Start with a small project. Build to bigger ones. I've known people and organizations for years before engaging at any meaningful level. Days and weeks just don't fly for anything more than pocket change.

8. Pray.

Don't do anything without taking time to pray. Never make quick decisions. Never trust your emotions or your heart.

Learn to hear God's voice and nudging, but I promise that will never come unless you learn to walk with Him first.

9. Walk with God.

God isn't anywhere near as interested in you doing things *for* Him, as He is in you doing things *with* Him.

If you don't know Him, don't enjoy spending time with Him, and don't live a life where your faith impacts who you are and the decisions you make on a daily basis, then you're the guy or gal I was talking about a few pages back.

You're doing things and helping people to make *you* feel better.

God's goal in the Great Commission was for us to go and make disciples, but we can't disciple anyone unless we're a disciple first.

Research specialist George Barna tells us that there's seven elements of spiritual formation that make up a true believer:

1. Worshipping God intimately and passionately.
2. Engaging in spiritual friendships with other believers.
3. Pursuing faith within the family.
4. Embracing intentional forms of spiritual growth.
5. Serving others.
6. Investing time and energy in spiritual things.
7. Having faith-based conversations with outsiders.

Apparently, I still have some work to do. I'm thinking there may be a couple others in the same boat.

Get your house in order, then come back. But in the meantime, stockpile your resources. You'll be glad you did. It still isn't yours.

10. Set clear guidelines and boundaries around what types of people/organizations God has led you to have a heart for through prayer and don't change lanes.

I want to help the world. Genuinely, I do. But I can't. I can't even help half of it. I can maybe help 0.0000000001 percent of it, so to do that I have to be focused on a specific group, a specific type of person or situation. For Linda and me, it's children and women in abusive and destructive situations.

Outside of these two focal areas, we say no 99 percent of the time. For the 1 percent we consider, there's usually exceptional circumstances as to why.

We've worked with organizations who had so few answers that we walked away even after completing successful projects with them. We've worked with organizations that we built relationships with over years, and when the time came to go big or go home, the details uncovered unnecessary spending, which caused us to go home.

Everyone's different, but what I've found particularly in faith-based organizations is that it's so easy to just put out a hand and ask for free money, they've gotten used to rationalizing in their minds what they do, why they do it, and how they do it, even when it makes no sense to anyone else.

As entrepreneurs, this is where it's our duty to use the intelligence and business smarts God has given us as a part of our training for His benefit, and stop the waste, stop the inefficiency, and start turning things around.

If you're wondering why you even need to get involved and who you're supposed to help, keep reading, Jesus had much to say about it. We're going there next.

CHAPTER 15
THE WHO

Shall we play a game?

If you know where that quote comes from, we're BFFs already. If you don't, go check out iTunes sometime and search for an eighties classic movie called *War Games* with Matthew Broderick. Once you stop laughing at the computing power of a device that was supposedly able to start global thermonuclear war, you can be wowed by the simplicity of a movie about a nerd, and hacking.

I'd like to play a game right now.

Here goes.

Would you like to buy a car from me for $50,000? No? You need more, right?

What if I told you it was brand new? Would that change your mind?

What if you could have any color you like? Still not convinced? Wondering why you can't just go buy a brand-new

Ford Mustang or Chevy Tahoe for less than $50k and pocket the change?

Okay, stay with me.

What if I told you it had leather inside complete with a full navigation system?

What if I told you it was a convertible?

Getting warmer?

Still not convinced if this is the bargain of a lifetime or I'm ripping you off?

What if I told you the seats massage you? Or how about reclining rear seats?

Still no? Okay, one more…

What if I told you it was a Rolls-Royce Phantom?

That did it, right? Those three little words changed everything because even if you don't know that's a $400,000 vehicle, you do know enough to know that anything called Rolls-Royce is luxury at its best. Whether you can afford it or not, finding $50,000 to buy one becomes a no-brainer. It's like that preacher who got cornered by a wily reporter asking why he needed to buy another jet when he already had a couple. "It was so cheap," he said, "it would have been wrong not to."

Wow.

The point of this exercise is that some things need decisions to be made.

Others make decisions for us.

Being generous and returning to God what's His falls into the second category. The only questions are how? To whom? When?

.   .   .

There was a man called George Müller who lived in the 1800s. He wasn't particularly special, didn't have millions of dollars in the bank, but as he grew, he realized that there were lots of boys and girls on the streets of London with no homes to go to.

He didn't get a bolt of lightning or an angel visitation, but he did wake up one day and decide that the Bible demanded he do something.

So he did.

Because no one else was.

He opened an orphanage in 1836. With zero training or experience with children.

History tells us that over the next sixty years he would care for over 10,000 orphans, build 117 schools and give free education to more than 120,000 children, (many of whom were orphans). This is almost two hundred years ago!

That's a whole bunch of kids.

Want to know something even crazier?

He never asked anyone for a dime.

Sure, he had supporters, people like you and me. But he only ever asked God for help. He was a pray-er.

Legend has it that one morning with no food in the children's home they continued with their normal routine, eventually sitting down and saying grace, thanking God for breakfast. As they finished praying, there was a knock at the door.

It was a baker.

Standing there with bread in his hand.

Enough for everyone.

In 1875 George was seventy years old when he decided it might be a good idea to travel the world for Jesus. He spent the next seventeen years traveling over 200,000 miles to Australia, Japan, China, America, and more, all by sea and land as airplanes didn't exist yet. He wanted to share what God was doing through his orphanages in England in the hope of encouraging others to seek God's will for their lives.

Then there's Bill. A twelve-year-old boy left on a street corner in Florida by his mom in 1960. She said she'd be back soon.

Three days later he was still waiting.

On the same step he'd been sitting the whole time.

She didn't come back.

A local, David Rudenis, noticed him and rather than "praying" about what to do, he figured he could do something, so he did. He took Bill in. He also paid for Bill to go to summer camp. That's when he heard about a God that loved him. He wanted in, so he went down to the altar, but no one would pray for him because he looked and smelled so bad. Standing there, he prayed to Jesus by himself.

"My mother doesn't want me; the Christians don't want me, but if you want me, here I am."

Years later Bill found out just how much God wanted him. He'd visited Brooklyn and been amazed by what he saw. He decided to take action and in 1979 moved to Bushwick, to do something for the kids living in a place that most people wanted to forget.

He founded an organization called Metro Ministries and over the next thirty years, what started as a kids' club for a handful of local boys and girls grew into something that touches the lives of over 20,000 kids aged twelve and under in New York.

And 250,000 kids each week around the world.

Every.

Single.

Week.

It's the largest Sunday school program in the world.

He's been shot, stabbed, beaten, and hospitalized numerous times, yet he continues to go back to the same streets so that those kids can experience being loved, and having hope as they continue to live in hopelessness and love-lessness.

The Black Eyed Peas had a smash hit song a few years back called "Where Is the Love?"

I think it's in Bushwick, New York.

And spreading.

The common thread for both of these folks is that they didn't wait for a sign. They didn't wait for God to speak. They recognized He's already spoken.

If you're waiting, it's time to stop.

You'll be waiting forever.

Sometimes, we just need to do something. Anything. Because if we don't, maybe no one else will either.

Jesus was out with His posse one day when some disciples of John the Baptist approached. John was in prison and starting to sweat about whether Jesus really was the Messiah or whether he'd blown it, and someone else was coming. Seeing as he was supposed to "prepare the way," I think he was wondering how successful he'd been because no one wants to enter heaven with a badge that should have five gold stars on it but actually has zero.

Jesus' response is telling.

He doesn't say yes, I'm the guy.

He goes with the practical.

The blind can see again. The lame are walking. Lepers are healed, the deaf can hear, and the dead have been brought back to life. Oh, and the good news has been shared with the poor.

His answer as to whether He is the Messiah or not is almost entirely based on practical, real-world needs and situations.

Good news comes in last place.

After He's helped people with their problems.

Ever noticed that telling a dead person God loves them doesn't get you very far? But if you bring them back to life first... Then you've got their attention.

When you read Scripture, it seems to overwhelmingly tell us that helping people practically is super important.

Isaiah tells us to:

"Learn to do right; seek justice. Defend the oppressed. Take up the cause of the fatherless; plead the case of the widow" (Isaiah 1:17).

"...and if you spend yourselves on behalf of the hungry, and satisfy the needs of the oppressed, then your light will rise in the darkness, and your night will become like the noonday" (Isaiah 58:10).

If we do what Isaiah is talking about, our night is supposed to become like noon. In other words, our darkest times will become our brightest.

I'd buy that for a dollar.

We see one of Jesus' disciples, John, talk about the same thing.

"If anyone has material possessions and sees a brother or sister in need but has no pity on them, how can the love of God be in that person?" (1 John 3:17)

I read verses like this and take them literally.

Because God inspired them.

Seeking justice, defending the oppressed, helping widows and orphans, feeding the hungry, etc. are all a given and need no further explanation. It's black and white. They're direct instructions.

Case closed.

Problem solved.

That's God talking right there.

To you.

And me.

Right now.

I don't see much about building more buildings or growing institutions. Do you? I see a lot about loving people. Helping people. Finding ways to get them out of the mess they're in so they can become who God made them to be.

That's the compass I've used to steer me as I look for projects to partner with or now begin planning my own. Outside of this, I stay away.

I wrote earlier that to do this well, takes time. It takes relationships, built over years and decades vs. weeks and months. I wasn't kidding. Walking alongside others, taking the time to learn and assess their situations, understand their value and what skills, competencies or "assets" they bring to the kingdom is the only effective way to deliver meaningful, lasting change.

There are no shortcuts that I've found that won't cost you.

We can't leave the folks we're looking to help out of the process either, because we need their buy-in. We need their engagement. Without it, based on the research completed by more than a few groups, we'll fail.

We'll also fail them.

The goal is to deliver impact and change with real outcomes that will stand the test of time. Impact that will continue to multiply and replicate itself long after we've "exited" the project, which would be self-sustaining by that point.

The only way to ensure this level of success is to reimagine the way we view missions work, outreach, and compassion, and redefine it within a modified and updated framework.

As you evaluate programs and projects, I'd suggest looking for three areas as a means of categorizing:

1. Relief— Help relief efforts the least, as they're immediate and temporary.
2. Rehabilitation— Better use of resources with longer lasting benefits.
3. Development— Best use of resources with the potential for permanent change and benefit.

The story of the good Samaritan would fall under *relief*. It was an urgent, immediate situation that was unavoidable. But very few situations measure up to this. Most should be catego-rized as *rehabilitation* if they're reactive in nature because they're rarely emergencies. Most proactive work would be cate-gorized as *development.*

If we're thinking about helping someone, or some group, it helps to make sure we really understand their hearts, plans, and abilities.

1. Is there really a crisis at hand?
2. To what extent did the individual(s) themselves cause or bring about the crises?
3. Are they able to help themselves out of the crises?
4. Have they been receiving help or support from others and if so, what does that look like and for how long?
5. Asset audit

View the localities and population as having value, some-thing to give, and something to contribute and start there. Use the "raw material" of the community and begin development from that place, rather than coming in as an outsider with all the answers to questions that people may not be asking.

Find local groups and partners already on the ground and look for ways to partner rather than reinventing the wheel. I never try to start something new if there's already someone doing something incredible in the same area as I'm exploring.

But the most important rule to learn.

The two things you need to tattoo on your forehead, so you look at them daily when you wake up are:

Don't do anything for someone else that they can do themselves.

Help those who want help AND are receptive to change.

No exceptions.

There's a delicate balance between outcomes vs. activities and production vs. process. Even thought leaders who agree on the major concepts we're discussing seem to veer away from each other on this issue.

On the one hand, as entrepreneurs and business-minded people we look for ROI, Return on Investment. We want to understand how *effective* our support and resources have been, not how *much* we gave. We're more concerned with the *outcome* vs. the *activity* in that sense, which doesn't sound like a bad thing.

However, we have to balance this with the reality that whoever is being helped is likely part of a community, and being helped by an organization that isn't run like a corporation. Not always because they don't have the skill or competence to, but because that's not the most effective way to operate.

We business builders work in hours and days, days and weeks, weeks and months. Lasting, impactful change, on the other hand, takes time.

Real time.

In other countries (if we look at overseas work) it takes even longer because they don't operate in time the way we do in the West. We've all heard jokes about "Africa Time" or "India Time," where the locals seem to have no sense of time.

In reality, they have a superb grasp on their time, they just choose to let time envelop them, rather than letting it rule them.

It's on purpose.

Yet it makes no sense to us.

If you're asking the question, "How can I fix this?", the answer is you can't. And you shouldn't.

They should. With your *help* and *support*.

If you're going to partner with other organizations, then donations should be made to legitimate, legally incorporated charities that have a proven, demonstrable track record of efficiency, integrity, and financial health as well as evidence of successful, developmental ministry.

Remember that whole "check them out" thing?

When you're conducting due diligence on a nonprofit to partner with and work alongside, they should have robust, effective financial and managerial systems in place for accountability.

JobsForLife.org in Raleigh, North Carolina, is a great example of a localized, workforce-based ministry that any mission-minded entrepreneur and business leader can connect with. By becoming a connector for people out of work, with others looking to hire, this professional, educational system helps *permanently* improve the *hireability* of its participants, while benefiting the businesses that hire them.

All wrapped within the truths and concepts found in Scripture.

All outside the walls of a building.

In the marketplace.

Where Jesus lived.

If you're interested in searching for and supporting other nonprofit organizations or charities, here's a few things you should be looking at:

1. Gospel-focused mission (because no change is meaningful or long lasting if it doesn't include the heart change that comes from salvation).
2. Operated through ABCD (asset-based community development) audits and processes to ensure they're truly utilizing the raw talent and resources God has already placed in the community.
3. Participation and leadership (or the seeds of leadership) from within the community, with the charity or nonprofit serving in a secondary or supportive role as opposed to a leadership role.

You may have heard the phrase microfinancing or microlending, made famous by Professor Mohammad Yunus. He won the Nobel Prize for his efforts, and I bring it up here because although not gospel focused, his ability to leverage the community and develop leadership from within it is legendary.

Years ago, he encountered a group of forty-two women in dire need in Bangladesh (Pakistan). Recognizing they needed rehabilitation and not relief (although they sometimes look similar) he chose not to give them, but to loan them twenty-seven dollars.

Twenty-seven.

You read that right.

In total.

For all forty-two of them.

When they repaid him, he started on the journey of building Grameen Bank, which now has over 8.4 million borrowers, 97 percent of whom are women, and has assets in the billions of dollars. It's never that simple though, and you should read about the mechanisms and systems they put into place to deliver those kinds of results. Peer group coaching and accountability coupled with intensive screening and vetting of potential borrowers are just a couple of ways that Yunus changed the game. They also changed the impact delivered along the way. Even now, a large loan to build housing for Grameen averages around three hundred US dollars.

Why are we talking about Yunus when we've just been peeling back the onion layers on partnering with great people, doing great things, in great ways, with great impact? Simple. Because that's just the baby step. That's just a glimpse. The real-life change comes next.

CHAPTER 16
A GLIMPSE

The New Testament has a concept called "firstfruits" that's mentioned in multiple places (James 1:18, Romans 8:23, 1 Corinthians 15:20 to get you started). In all of them it's used symbolically. It's misunderstood a bunch and misquoted even more because some folks think the word only applies to the Old Testament and the T-bomb.

It's way better than that.

When Jesus left, He promised to send us "another helper" (John 14:16). The original language is a little funky but essentially it means "another one like him, to help." Not help like a maid or cleaner who does things for us that we could do ourselves, help like Jesus who did something for us we could never do for ourselves. Paul expands on this (Romans 8:23) where he talks about the arrival of the Holy Spirit as a firstfruits. We know he's not being literal, it's about the Holy Spirit being a foretaste of the more to come.

• • •

It's a translation issue (not from Greek to English but from ancient use of language to our present day). The "firstfruits" wasn't it.

He was a deposit.

An installment.

A guarantee that more was coming.

More of the same.

Think of it like a deposit on a vehicle when you're car shopping. If you put a thousand dollars down, it's a firstfruits. It's your guarantee that more is coming.

More money, not bananas.

More of exactly what I gave you. It's my promise that complete payment will be made.

When Paul wrote that letter to his friends in Rome, he talked about God's spirit in those terms to encourage them that one day, in the new heaven and new earth, we'll experience not just a part of God's presence and Spirit, but all of it. The rest of it. More of the same.

I like to think of this firstfruits concept as a "glimpse." As though we're viewing a glimpse into what's coming, or God's seeing a glimpse of what's coming from us when we give Him our firstfruits. He gets the firstfruits from our hearts and our minds, when we've made a decision to do something, to give something back, long before we ever touch it.

The neat thing about glimpses is that God uses them in our lives too. To show us things about our future selves. About what He might be up to as He works in our lives.

Remember that time I met a girl and went preaching to India the day after our first date? You know. The one.

Well, a little before then, when I was figuring out how to be the next Billy Graham, I enrolled myself into a little church-based Bible college, attending two days each week when I wasn't working. I wasn't the most studious of the group, but I got my work done in the evenings, even without Zoom.

I met some incredible folks at that college, one of whom was the big cheese himself, we'll call him Frank. Frank was Australian and married to a Malaysian (that's what happens when you go be a missionary somewhere, I guess). He was a super-likeable guy, but it was pretty obvious that this college principal gig wasn't a high-paying job. I don't know how his car started each day, but it looked like the Toyota truck from *Top Gear* after they'd tried to destroy it for multiple seasons.

As things got serious for Linda and me, we decided we'd go study theology together at a full-time college the next year, so we started making plans and packing. We didn't have a whole lot of money, so keeping my car running, insured, and gassed seemed like mission impossible. Selling it made way more sense, but then I had an idea.

Even though I made peanuts, as two broke, wannabe students we made a decision together that would be a glimpse of a future we'd never dreamed of.

"What if we don't sell the car and just give it to Frank instead?" I said. It became clear quickly that we were both thinking the same thing.

Then the doubts started.

How can you do that?

You need the money from a car sale to help pay for school.

It's a perfectly good car, you could park it in the garage for three years, graduate, and still have a great vehicle waiting for you when you get back.

My mind wouldn't stop, but it felt like the right thing to do. Someone needed help. I was in a place where I could help. So no-brainer. It's all God's anyway, right?

We settled it together and that was that. We were going to trust God had our backs for the future. I still remember the day I drove it over there with one of my buddies in tow. We stopped to fill up (at $7/gallon in 1994) and my friend was super perplexed. "Dude, you're giving him a car, why spend another fifty dollars? He can gas it up."

He was right. I was paying more than I made in a whole day of work to gas it up when I didn't need to. But it's in moments like these that you have the freedom to decide whether you're going to put a cherry on top or not.

I like cherries. Especially on a Chick-fil-A milkshake.

I figured if I'm going to do something, I'm doing it right. Today we'd say, "You go big, or you go home."

We went big.

I'd love to tell you that when we graduated God showed up with a free car back for us. He didn't. The car we bought was less of a car, older and with more miles than the one we'd given away. My mind had been right. We'd have been better off just sticking the old one in storage for three years.

It was the first of a run of old dogs, not one of which cost more than maybe a couple thousand dollars.

Looking back, the glimpse was the lesson. God was developing a generous spirit in our hearts, knowing where He wanted to take us.

Do you have any glimpses like that in your life? Look back and think through moments of life, to see if God has shown you a glimpse, a firstfruits of something that could be a deposit of more to come.

I believe God was demonstrating His principle of firstfruits in me that day. That what comes first is the same in nature as what comes later. God uses these nudges or signs to show us something in our hearts that grows and becomes more visible as the years go by.

They're glimpses of the giftings and callings He's placed over our lives and so we need to pay attention if we don't want to miss them.

If we learn to discern, paying attention to these things, we'll find the road ahead clearer, easier, and more peaceful. If we don't, we'll continue to see the same lessons come up again and again until we recognize that God is trying to get our attention.

My journey really started when I was around twelve years old and picked up my first job. I'd work the flea markets on Saturday mornings and evenings for around five dollars. After a few months of doing a solid job (which really just meant showing up and sticking it out), I received my first ever pay increase. From five dollars to seven.

Back then, I didn't know the T-bomb was a cuss word, so I'd been giving God my fifty cents and feeling pretty good about it.

Your journey might be a little different. You might not have grown up with giving as a part of your lives so this may all sound a little strange. It also may feel a little foreign when you start to do it.

Don't panic. Baby steps.

It's easy when it's fifty cents. It's harder when it's fifty grand.

It shouldn't be.

But I'm human. And selfish.

I'm still holding out for that boat.

The beauty of this chapter is that I don't want your money. There's no ulterior motive here. Just a genuine desire to help you see the amazing gift God's given you, through your business and entrepreneurial endeavors.

The success He's blessed you with was never about you, and never for you.

It was about Him.

For Him.

He's calling us to a place where we recognize His ownership over everything, along with His incredible grace to bring us into His plans, while allowing us to be a part of the solution the world needs. Starting with your neighborhood, your community, or even your family.

The journey of generosity starts now and ends in eternity. There's no destination here on earth, just a more exciting path, with bigger mountains to climb, and bigger rewards to come.

Every now and again I'll listen to one of my favorite blasts from the past, I mentioned him earlier, Keith Green. He died at twenty-eight years old, having been a Christian for around three to four years yet over twenty-five years later his music still speaks to a new generation.

His style was edgy. He set new standards for the word "direct" and never minced his words when singing. He believed his music was a ministry and so, while recognized as the most popular Christian recording artist of his day, he decided to go visit his record label and ask if they'd release him from his contract.

Why?

So he could record new material and give it away for free.

You read that right.

Free.

Wait, why?

Because he wanted as many people as possible to hear about Jesus.

One of my favorite songs is called "To Obey Is Better Than Sacrifice" and the line that resonated with me like a bowl of milk to a Cheshire cat was this:

"I don't need your money; I want your life."

He was trying to show us that from God's perspective, giving our time is more important than money, even if giving money does help.

As entrepreneurs, we get this. If you're successful, you really get this.

Because you have no time.

Neither do I.

But God wants our time.

Something has to give.

And it's not God.

I know money makes the world go round. I know that giving money does things that nothing else can, but it's not enough. Although helping people or organizations financially is a great thing to do, God needs more than that. So do we.

We know money is a commodity. Something you can

always get more of. Time is something entirely different because we can NEVER get it back, no matter what we do. We get one chance to make the most of any minute in our lives and that's it. When we choose to give it away, we're making the ultimate sacrifice for Jesus.

We're showing Him that we're unselfish.

Giving our time changes us on the inside because we're putting others before ourselves. We're making a conscious decision to choose something bigger and more important than us. We're making a conscious decision to stop being selfish, to stop focusing on our own world and instead, focus on God's.

The Bible tells us we were created in the image of God. Have you noticed how much God loves to engage and love on others? He did it from the beginning and if we're supposed to be in His image, then we should too. God gave His time, six days out of seven, to build something for us. If we're made in His image… Well, you get it.

The Bible tells us God is love.

He doesn't do love.

He isn't loving.

He simply *is* love.

The doing and loving are outward manifestations of His *being* love.

We didn't know we needed help, but God did. So He sent Jesus. There are people out there who don't know they need help, you know, the ones we read about in Isaiah and John earlier. God's sending us out to them in the same way. And in the same way Jesus didn't just do everything for everyone but instead engaged His local community (the disciples, His followers) by sending them out to minister, we need to do the same.

We can start with the single mom with four kids, struggling with a shopping cart full of groceries as we walk into the store. Maybe a few minutes lost to help her is sowing a firstfruits? What about the broken-down vehicle at the roadside? Maybe a few minutes lost to help is what Jesus would do?

When we apply it to money, something interesting happens. When you make $100,000, giving away $20,000 seems like a lot.

When you hit $1m, giving away $200,000 doesn't seem as much. You've still got $800,000 left instead of $80,000.

When you hit $10m, giving away $2m is nothing. You'll be fine with the other $8m. Yet somehow, it feels harder, because it's more.

The more successful we are, the easier it should become to give money away but the harder it is to give away time. That's why God wants your time too. Because He wants all of you, knowing when that happens, it brings about change that only God can bring, through the experiences we have as we give away those moments. Who wants to be around a selfish person anyway?

Looking back to see glimpses is great. Recognizing those firstfruits in our lives is super important to help us understand the future God has mapped out for us. But part of that future is moving beyond partnering, beyond supporting, and beyond giving only money, and arriving at the next level, where we pour rocket fuel on our businesses and see liftoff. I call it achieving B.O.O.M. And we're going to talk about it now. Because this is the moment you were made for, or if you're an aspiring entrepreneur who hasn't found success yet, then don't panic, this is the moment you're aiming for. The moment you experience all the freedom and release from letting go and giving back to God everything you have and everything you are.

It's when we realize that drive for excellence, professionalism, and all the focus, energy, and effort it took was worth it, because it was to build a gift for Jesus, that's far more than the frankincense or myrrh those three kings brought Him.

Now you're the king, I'm the king, and we're the kings bringing Him our gifts, understanding that our very lives are part of what He hopes for.

Are you ready to step up and join me as we map out the ministry of business?

CHAPTER 17
B.O.O.M.

I've been making a case that the current model isn't working. Churches and nonprofits are burning time, energy, and resources on finding donors and managing donors instead of doing the work they set out to do.

They can't help it.

They don't have the money, so they need ours.

It's the model that's in motion and its been failing for decades. No matter how hard you ask, no matter how heart-warming the stories to pull on the heartstrings, there's only so much they can hope to receive.

Then you've got the folks who abuse good people and think the donations coming in are theirs to spend.

They're wrong, and they're going to find that out one day.

I won't be standing next to them.

Because they might be with the other guy, in his playground.

You know, the hot one.

A system where people have ideas they can't execute on or fund without a six-month capital campaign seems crazy. If God has an idea that He passes along to us, doesn't it make more sense for Him to pass it along to someone who is in a position to handle it? To someone who can simply take care of it and make it a reality?

In the least amount of time and the most efficient way possible?

It's not that anyone is wrong here and I'm not pooping on anyone's parade. It's simple practicality. The current model exists because we failed. We didn't listen to God when He spoke, because we stopped realizing that He speaks to all of us. We've just been leaving it to the pros.

We didn't act when God nudged, despite having what was needed to get the job done. We didn't step up, either because we were too busy or because we figured someone else would. Our stubbornness resulted in Him finding others with great hearts who would.

But make no mistake.

They're the alternate team.

The folks who were never meant to play on the field but were supposed to coach others that would.

Us.

But we weren't on the field. We didn't even know where the field was. So they had to step up and play in our place.

He drafted them because we entrepreneurs got so focused on our success, and buying stuff, that we neglected His purpose and mission for our lives and for our businesses.

The great news is that it's time for change, and change is coming.

Look around at how many groups are springing up around this same idea, this same concept, of God using business to impact His marketplace. More than that, look at how He's fusing business with a mission to deliver exponentially more.

We talked a little about "asset-based community development" earlier (ABCD for short). The concept was developed by John L. McKnight and John P. Kretzmann at Northwestern University. In 1993 they published a book called *Building Communities from the Inside Out* that explains how asset-based community development as a methodology delivers the sustainable development of communities based on their strengths and potentials. It involves assessing the resources, skills, and experience available in any given community, and then organizing that community around issues that move its members into action. Only from that point, they argue, can we then determine and take any appropriate action.

Their logic is that for change to work, buy-in is needed. Buy-in from the locals, who've been around a long time, and will continue to be around for a long time more. Sounds a little like business, don't you think? Small, local businesses tend to stick around in their communities for a while, making them the perfect vehicle to drive change and impact for the kingdom.

By using the community's own assets and resources as the basis for development, their framework empowers the people of the community by encouraging them to utilize what they already possess. We come alongside to highlight what they can't see, support them as they attempt to bring about change, and cheer as they succeed.

The only time outside resources are brought in is when local resources aren't sufficient to solve whatever the major needs of the community are. Even then, caution is needed so nothing happens in a way that undermines or sidesteps the local initiatives.

We're never going to do things for the poor people in a community. Instead, we're going to do things with them.

Jehovah Jireh Church in Manila took this idea and built something called an SCA (savings and credit association). Don't worry, I didn't know what that was either.

Rather than do what churches typically do, looking to raise funds and distributing them freely, they recognized the need for a different approach because they had no donors to raise funds from!

Most of their congregation are poor.

The SCA created a framework to fix this.

Each member deposits twenty cents (yes, cents) per week so the group can make interest-bearing loans to other members. They are also required to deposit an additional five cents per week into an emergency fund which is distributed separately, but again, only to members of the SCA. As most of the members earn between one to five dollars per day, these amounts aren't insignificant.

If someone becomes sick (or a family member), they're eligible to borrow from the emergency fund at zero percent interest up to a maximum amount equal to whatever they've paid in personally. In other words, if Shirley has paid in a total of two dollars (twenty cents per week over ten weeks), then the most she can borrow is two dollars.

They can only borrow for medical emergencies that are unforeseeable (childbirth wouldn't count as in the eyes of the SCA it is foreseeable, for about nine months, giving plenty of time to save and prepare).

Similarly, if you need to borrow money for groceries or a utility bill you'd be denied, as these are all avoidable, plannable expenses and not emergencies. We talked about this earlier when we discussed the differences between relief and rehabilitation when planning our giving.

This SCA model is a fascinating example of using business and entrepreneurial principles to impact the marketplace and change lives.

The fact that it works so well proves the point.

It also has an incredibly high participation and repayment rate.

Maria was a member of that church. Her child would have died had it not been for the help available through the loan she received. As she tells the story, the funds weren't the only benefit here. She also talked about how the group prayed for her and visited her child.[1]

This is a great example of the fusion of business and mission.

Although SCAs don't need ongoing donations or support from outside, they do need someone or some entity to set them up in the first place. From there, they're completely self-sustaining.

Run by and managed by their own members.

They work.

When a Business Operates On Mission its impact expands beyond revenues and profits. God sprinkles His magical fairy dust on it to deliver a formula that looks something like this:

$1+1=11$.

It's not a linear equation and doesn't make sense to us, because we live and operate in a limited capacity, within a limited universe.

God doesn't.

By its very definition and reason for existence, a business multiplies what we put in to deliver gains that we call profit.

It was always a multiplication formula.

Never addition.

There isn't one way to do this, but my heart is to share the way I've tried to figure this journey out. I'm bringing you into my bubble, so you can see what we've been trying in the hopes you can learn from it, and then go out and do better. It's why connecting with others like us and building our community is key.

When we take our businesses and fuse them with faith, with the Great Commission, recognizing the call of God on that union, it's like pouring rocket fuel onto the launchpad and priming the ignition.

An explosion occurs.

Exponential returns happen.

You can almost hear the boom.

That's the sound of Jesus smiling. If He made sounds when He smiled. Which He probably doesn't, but what if He did?

We hear venture capitalists and angel investors talk about

needing 10x returns but God only asked for a 2x return in the story of the talents and stewards. I know I know, Jesus walked in Israel, but in Texas everything's bigger. Okay, you win, we can stick with 10x.

When we started WorkLodge we had no idea what to do. So we created a 501(c)3 organization, thinking this would allow us to build margin from year to year in a tax-efficient way as we looked for projects and people to partner with, until we arrived at the ultimate place of creating our own.

Partnerships are great.

They're valuable.

They connect you to amazing people, and they allow you to reach beyond your current capacity and join with others to do things you'd never dreamed of.

But there's another level.

A level of influence, impact, and innocence that some of us arrive at that calls for more. A level where capital and resources aren't enough. A level that demands all of us, and all of our teams.

As we grow our business and build our teams, we need to hire and build not just for our core business, but for God's business too, the business of changing lives and saving people.

We need to build depth and capability by hiring for a future that understands our team won't spend forty hours each week on the business alone. Each member should be willing and able to commit some of that time to kingdom business.

The mission that God has placed on *your* heart.

To help grow and build something that *you* can sustain.

That *your* business can build.

Can your team help the locals in an African village sell something or do something? They don't just need funding, they need teaching. They need connections. Infrastructure. Shipping. Distribution. Mentorship. All things you may be able to facilitate, supported by your team of employees in your day-to-day business.

When we lean into the strongest gifts God gave us and align them with the strongest gifts of those who work for us, we suddenly create a team that can play on the field of Marketplace.

Got an outstanding marketing guru in-house?

Great. God needs his talent.

Got an outstanding operations genius on the team?

God needs their talent also.

ALL of your business is His. In a literal sense. All of your business can put a dent in the world, creating impact and changing lives, but only if you'll allow it to, by leaning into His call and mission.

I'm right here with you, so let's look at how easy this is.

A few months ago, we were recording a podcast episode with an awesome lady in Thailand, who's rescuing human trafficking victims and retraining them to give them skills, hope, and a real tangible, alternative way to make a living.

But it's not enough to rescue them. If that's all we do, then what? Where do they go next? What do they do for income? This is the key to sustainable, impactful, entrepreneurial missions. We don't simply help. We help build systems and infrastructure so our finished product will be self-sustaining, and the training wheels can come off.

As we chatted, we found out that they were developing a new program around textiles, around the creation of products like super-cool beanie hats.

But they had a problem.

They had plenty of labor, but only one sewing machine.

A crappy one at that.

You know where this is going, right?

"What would happen if you had another sewing machine?" I asked.

"More women could make more products faster, which we could sell to generate more income for them," was the reply.

"How many sewing machines do you need?"

"Two."

Two.

Seriously?

They're struggling to help others because they can't afford a couple of sewing machines? If you're anything like me, you're not okay living in a world like that. It was easy for me to write the check, but I want to live in a place where no check ever needs to be asked for.

It's easy for us to be the savior of the day, but we should never need to be, because Jesus already took that spot.

He's built us and our business for "such a time like this" to quote the ancient Queen Esther. This is our time to rise up, to re-evaluate, restructure, and redefine the businesses we've built and operate.

If your gift is to build businesses, run businesses, and grow teams, then why feel guilty or ashamed of that?

It's what God made you to do.

You were created for exactly that purpose.

Not to serve on an usher team.

Not to volunteer three hours a week at the soup kitchen handing out bread.

Although those things are good, you were made for more.

And He expects it.

The more successful we are, moving from seven figures and up in profit, the more likely it is that God expects us to bring all impact mission efforts in-house. Whether through our for-profit business, or by creating our own nonprofit organizations.

At that level, our skills and competencies combined with the breadth of talent in our team scream for us to lead the charge in areas we sense God nudging in our lives. We put boots on the ground. Hiring smarter and better. We attract the talent, because they want to be surrounded by excellence, but also success.

Look for those glimpses in your past that show as firstfruits of where God could be leading your heart. Find your passion, what God's laid on your heart, and look for specific people groups to start with.

Is it digging wells for clean water?

Is it adoption from either inside or outside the US?

Is it helping kids?

Or helping widows?

For us, it's the overlooked in society.

Children without homes, without parents, without hope.

Women in abusive situations like sex trafficking and slavery.

It's overwhelmingly any mission that takes the gospel to

others, because without Jesus, nothing matters eternally anyway.

Whatever it is for you, be confident that you have everything needed to make it become reality. A larger bench to lean on, at the sidelines of the playing field where your team is in action.

If you import products from Asia, perhaps God has other doors to open up for you? Next time you're out there, add a few extra days onto your trip and see what God does.

My amazing wife, Linda, does our mission-related trips for us because I pretty much fit into an airplane seat like Shaquille O'Neal fits into a Mini. It might be possible with a little effort, but practically it's not the best idea.

She flew out to Cambodia with two of our kids a few years back (we include them in most projects because we want them to grow up seeing this Business + Mission formula in action). On the plane, she heard a loud voice coming from the row in front. She's no snoop, but he was talking so loudly and enthusiastically she leaned forward to hear what he was saying.

Turns out he was a Hollywood stuntman.

He'd been involved in some major movies but when he found himself in Cambodia filming, he fell in love with the country.

At the same time, he couldn't help but notice how poor the people were, and how many of them didn't have clean water.

Sensing that nudge, he figured he'd do something about it.

He talked off the ear of the guy sitting next to him for what seemed like hours, but he had no idea God had another listener sitting one row back.

We've built quite a few wells with Shane since then. Providing clean water to thousands of people in villages across the country. One of the neat things about clean water is that it isn't just used for drinking. They use it to farm because the rivers are so polluted. As a result, the vegetables and flowers grow stronger, quicker, and better, which helps them sell quicker at the market.

The water fuels their enterprise.

It's not the ultimate solution, but a partial solution, that feeds into other issues while resolving them too.

Without Jesus you're helping people.

Which is awesome.

With Jesus you have the opportunity to transform people.

Which is even more awesome.

We help folks no matter what, but let your heart and your drive come from your relationship with Him because that's where we'll find the guidance we need for the mission, and for our businesses.

Walk closer with Him today than you did yesterday, always remembering that He wants you still more than He wants you busy. He wants your heart more than He wants your life.

One of the reasons I believe God designed this formula of Business + Mission to deliver impact is because He knew that entrepreneurs, the kings of today, have learned how to execute.

No one builds a successful, profitable business by accident.

Sure, you might get lucky for a few months, but sustainable, consistent growth doesn't come without skill. Skill that He birthed inside of you when He made you in His image.

Because He's an entrepreneur too.

Creating things out of nothing is His specialty. Funnily enough it's the mantra of entrepreneurship too.

Many years ago, I wrote a course that included a definition of success for believers I found online. It's still super relevant today and helps bring some perspective to the road ahead for each one of us so I quoted part of it below. Whether we're making hundreds of thousands in profit, or millions, it still works.

What matters is:

- *Not simply how many people come to our church services, but how many people our churches serve.*
- *Not simply how many people attend our ministry, but how many people we have equipped for ministry.*
- *Not simply how many people minister inside the church, but how many minister outside the church.*
- *Not simply helping people become more whole themselves, but helping people bring more wholeness to their world (i.e., justice, healing, relief).*
- *Not simply how many ministries we start, but how many ministries we help.*
- *Not simply how many unbelievers we bring into the community of faith, but how many "believers" we help experience a healthy community.*
- *Not simply counting the resources that God gives us to steward but counting how many good stewards we are developing for the sake of the world.*
- *Not simply how we are connecting with our culture but how we are engaging our culture.*

- *Not simply how much peace we bring to individuals, but how much peace we bring to our world.*
- *Not simply how effective we are with our mission, but how faithful we are to our God.*
- *Not simply how unified our local church is, but how unified "the church" is in our neighborhood, city, and world.*
- *Not simply how many people we bring into the kingdom, but how much of the kingdom we bring to the earth.*[2]

Your ministry is twofold. Its two sides of the same coin. You minister to your team, your customers, and your vendors or partners by living out your faith in your day-to-day world. You then give from the profits generated to activate the mission work by either partnering and supporting others you've researched or using your skills and intellect, and maybe even your team and business, to find new ways to deliver what God is placing on your heart directly.

---

1. https://dci.org.uk/bankingnotes/
2. https://jrwoodward.com/

CHAPTER 18
NOW WHAT?

There was a famous preacher born in South India a long time ago. As a baby, he was saved one night when his parents noticed a deadly cobra wriggling under his blanket as he lay in his crib. He was unharmed, so they thought perhaps God had protected him for a reason, and as he grew, it was clear that he was very different from his playmates.

He was extremely helpful to everyone in the village, unselfish and frequently bringing beggars home to be fed by his parents—though they often scolded him for his unwarranted generosity! He also led his classmates in devotionals before school!

A golden child, right?

He grew up to be one of the most famous men in India, preaching Jesus Christ. Despite most of India being Hindu, and worshipping millions of gods, he once said:

"Follow Jesus Christ. His words must be imprinted on your hearts, and you must resolve to practice all that he taught. We are true Christians only when we live according to the teachings of Jesus and practice them."

He wasn't afraid of the establishment and has been credited by thousands of eyewitnesses to be highly successful in the miraculous. He healed thousands of people from all types of sickness, some of whom traveled across the world to see him. He has been the subject of countless books, yet outside of India he is little known except to those who have stumbled across him. He has even raised the dead more than once.

He also seemed to be gifted in materializing things out of nothing that someone would then eat or drink to bring about a healing.

Wait.

What?

Right. It's getting weird now, no?

Was this something new that God was doing? We could absolutely put this down to the spiritual gift of miracles, but we'd be wrong. His name was Sai Baba, and he didn't just claim to be sent from God, he claimed that he was a god.

This is my final warning for us to trust less in others, and what other people say or claim, and to lean into Jesus ourselves, learning to listen and hear His voice and His nudges. As a priest and king, you were made for this. Through this book, we've taken a journey through time to prove this.

With Gideon, we saw how God interacted with him and he with God. How his self-awareness worked against him because he viewed himself through his past whereas God viewed him through his future. We saw God command him to step up and lead an army, when he'd never led one before, and we saw God honor that faith, rewarding him with success.

We've talked about Jesus' story of the sheep and the goats, understanding that despite both groups being believers, one group didn't make it into Jesus' home for no other reason than what they did and didn't do.

We've dug deep into God's example as an entrepreneur (along with Jesus' and Paul's), clearly demonstrating that business IS ministry, and is *the* ministry we were created for whether as a leader or as part of the team. Connected to this is the marketplace-first perspective that is very much closer in alignment with Jesus' life than anything else, given most of His ministry and teaching also happened in the marketplace, outside the walls of a building and the confines of an institution.

We've looked at the differences between today's pastors and entrepreneurs, highlighting the reality that their worlds, focus, and causes are mostly different, while suggesting that perhaps it's the entrepreneur's call and leading that should be followed (the mission-related part) while trusting that God provides to the ones with the resources to fulfill it instead of the other way around.

We've begun to embrace the idea that true stewardship isn't found in the hollow words of the mantra "It's all God's anyway," but rather in living out those words through intentionality and choices. Only by making hard decisions that involve sacrifice on our part can we find our way to truly live out this concept, but that likely means a smaller house, fewer cars, fewer toys, and more for Jesus.

We looked at models of generosity that hopefully stirred your heart to think about where you fall on the elasticity of generosity scale. Zero percent to one hundred percent is the range and we all need to prayerfully consider at what stage we find ourselves at, understanding that it will evolve over time.

We dug deeper into the idea that helping can sometimes hurt, recognizing the need to understand the ramifications of our decisions all the way through to the end. Simply feeling good about the fact that we did *something isn't enough.*

We talked about glimpses and firstfruits, to help learn that this methodology is often used by God to capture our attention, to show us things in baby steps, early in our lives, because He knows we need to build up to the greatness that He's put inside each one of us.

We pulled on the thread of spiritual warfare. A theological concept that explains the Enemy and his work in our world, constantly working against us to hinder and thwart God's best for our lives. This wasn't to scare, but to enlighten us and ensure we will be better prepared when those situations come.

Finally, we talked about what a Business Operating On Mission (B.O.O.M.) looks like, recognizing the forgotten formula of Scripture: Business + Mission = B.O.O.M., or explosive impact for God's kingdom.

So now what?

If you're asking that question, you're not alone.

First, although saving and building wealth for future generations is an acceptable track for us to run on in God's eyes, it's not the primary or ultimate track for us to focus on. The Bible clearly tells us to store up our treasure in heaven, not on earth. It's another tension we need to navigate to get the balance right, but if we model our generosity along the suggestions made earlier, we should find ourselves in a good place to get the balance right.

If you're early in the process, just starting or growing a business, God's expectations on you and your life may be different, they may be less, but they're still there.

Stretch yourself for Him.

Push yourself to begin thinking now about how to evolve and shape your entrepreneurial journey to include Him and His mission, each and every week.

If you're further along, seeing success and generating profit, it's time to step up. It's time to rethink the balance and begin putting intentional effort and resources into the mission He's put on your heart.

Not someone else's mission.

Your mission.

Waiting until your profit and revenue increase before you start means you've already failed. But tomorrow's a new day. Make it different.

The whole point of stepping out in faith means giving first and learning to hear God's voice so you can trust Him. Look at those glimpses in your life and build on them. Start there and grow. Use every tool in your toolshed. Pull from the strengths of your staff. Hire more staff if you need to but go out there and make it happen.

Something.

Anything.

It's your calling, and now you know there's no excuses.

If you're a church leader or pastor, I love your heart and I love what you're trying to do. We aren't at odds with each other, but the model you're backing isn't God's plan A. Adapt and change. . Look for leaders, for those entrepreneurs with God's gifting and calling on their lives and don't try to shape them, remold them, or change them. Embrace them with their flaws.

Love on them.
Pray for them.
Empower them.
Enable them.

Support them and get interested in what God's doing through *them* rather than trying to get them interested in what you think God's trying to do through you. You'll tag along for the ride of your life and be part of an amazing revival that's coming to the world through this original plan. By doing that, you'll also see your heart's desires being fulfilled at the same time.

Haven't you noticed that everything's changing?

That means the church is changing too.

The organic church.

Small *c*.

We worship more outside of buildings now than we ever have. We listen to more encouragement and messages about Jesus outside than in. It's the same for community, and it's all because of business, what it brings and what it can create.

Technology is reimagining who we as a church are, and what we can do.

We're able to build connected communities outside the walls and millions of people are signing up. Looking to engage. Looking for tribes to join, because as humans, we were made in God's image, an image of community.

We're leveraging technology to further the kingdom delivering outcomes and impact that would have been thought impossible just a decade ago.

It's only possible because of business.

Because an entrepreneur had an idea.

But what other ideas are out there waiting to be thought of? What other ideas are out there that God wants to communicate to someone who can't hear? Could you be the voice? Could you be the conduit? Could you help them grow to the point they can hear directly from Him, which is the ultimate goal anyway?

The old model has already been trashed. Let's not go dumpster diving hoping to dig it back out. A faith built around Sunday mornings and Wednesday nights doesn't work. We need a faith that's worked out daily, which means we need our coaches daily too.

We don't need teams of leaders standing ready at fixed times of the week because we aren't operating on that timetable anymore. Why would we stop what we're building to drive across town on a Wednesday night, losing time, burning energy, and costing money, when we can fit that time of ministry around our schedule thanks to a phone?

What about community, I hear you asking? Great question, because I get more community from my neighborhood Facebook group than I do attending a Wednesday night service. My podcaster group is thousands, and I can connect with any of them at any time.

My men's group is the same.

We're not here to fund buildings and expenses. Jesus wasn't either.

The American church receives around $150 billion each year in donations and spends $90 billion of it on buildings and staff.

That's just the American church.

In one year.

I'm not really sure where the other $60 billion goes.

The UN says that we could immediately eliminate world hunger for $116 billion.

So no one else has to die from starvation, malnutrition, or other related illnesses.

I don't know about you, but after reading the sheep and the goats I'm betting Jesus would go for world hunger while still having $34 billion left.

I hear you can still do quite a lot with that.

My hope and prayer as you finish this book is that you've realized there's a better way, it's the only way to bring change to the world, and it's God's original way, hidden in His formula of Business + Mission = B.O.O.M.

You're a rock star. It's not too late and the clock starts now. I heard it once said that you can keep everything you can fit in your coffin, but only what you can pack *after* you pass away.

Let's live that out now, investing more into His kingdom than ours each and every year.

As you now look to find ways to fuse business with mission in your life, in your business, and in your team, I would love to hear the stories, and be of help in any way I can. Connect with me at www.mikethakur.com.

My hope is that pastors and church leaders would thoughtfully consider the arguments I've put forth. My wish is that kids growing up and parents raising them would begin to recognize the unlimited power and opportunity for the Great Commission to be fulfilled through entrepreneurship and steer their kids into a life of impact. My prayer is that business owners would do business God's way, live like the kings they were created to be, not kings who excel in excess, but kings who understand that they're subject to the King of kings and His goals, His mission, particularly in relation to the business He's trusted them with.

Ultimately, I hope to see you out there on the field, playing the game, because it's big enough for us all, and that's how we change the world.

APPENDIX: LET'S DO THIS

As I've written this book and spoken to others about the ideas presented, one of the most common questions asked is "Ok, but what *exactly* should I do next?". Although the answer varies, the steps necessary have some similarities.

Essentially, you have four choices as a reader at this point:

1. Do nothing.

Keep the status quo and carry on as if nothing has changed.

2. Give a little, give a lot.

If you aren't a giver on a regular basis, this might seem like the way to start or if you are a giver, you may be thinking it's time to step it up and do more. Either way, baby steps are ok. Stretching your faith no matter what level it's at is never a bad thing.

3. Take the lead.

Find your glimpse. Dig deep in your heart and look back to identify what God has been showing you over the years you've experienced life. Don't limit yourself to only the years you've been a believer. If God put something on your heart before you decided to follow Him, that could still be the area He destined for you to touch.

Once you've found your glimpse, lean into it. Embrace the challenge and step up.

4. Chase self-sustainability.

It's great to lead the charge and it's awesome to bring your experience, your resources, your staff and your network into the fold, utilizing each wherever possible for maximum impact and benefit for the mission.

But it's not enough.

You need to do more.

And that more is to lead and build something that can sustain itself, reproduce itself, and multiply. That's the place when B.O.O.M. becomes real.

But what does that look like?

Let's get a little more granular.

To truly achieve 3 & 4, just like any entrepreneurial journey, you're going to need to research, and learn, there's no difference if you want to succeed. You don't start a business unless it's something you're good at, you know about and you truly believe you can bring something new to the market. This is no different.

If building clean water wells is where your heart finds itself and you're ready to step up and build 1000, then here's how I'd approach that.

First, I'd think about the region of the world I could best serve. It might be Africa, because I've felt God's calling there for years. It might be India, because I have heritage there in my family tree. It might be South America, because it's closer and more manageable from Houston, Texas, where I live. Wherever it is, it has to be somewhere, and it needs to be specific, because most countries are big. So just saying Africa (which is a continent anyway) isn't specific enough. You'd need to say Uganda.

You need to settle on a place that fits because once you know where, you can start your market research!

Is the market there?

Is the need truly real?

Is the solution deliverable? Affordable? Logistically possible?

Is the market saturated already?!

If you find others already working in that area then great. Find the ones specifically addressing the needs your heart leans towards. Are they doing what you want to do and are they doing it well? Reach out and connect. Learn more about what they do and how they do it. Do all the things we know as entrepreneurs to do when we're conducting our market research on the viability of a new business location, or product line.

If you're satisfied with what you learn, go out there and visit. See what they're doing. See how they're doing it. Learn from their strengths and make note of any deficits. Then ask yourself two simple questions:

1. Should I be working with this group instead of starting something myself?
2. Could I do this better / faster / smarter than they are?

Check out their form 990 (this is the annual tax filing that's public record and outlines the major financials you'll want to see). Every charity that has 501(c)3 status in the United States has to file one. If they're small and their revenues are under $200,000 (along with assets of less than $500,000) then they file an EZ form that has little to no detail. Over $200,000 in revenue each year means filing the full form which is complex, detailed and incredibly helpful for us.

If they're spending 50% of their income on salaries, stay away. If they're already raising tens of millions of dollars each year, I'd ask myself if my input, whether financial or skill based, will really move the needle and bring any kind of meaningful change / improvement.

As a side note, one of the biggest issues with this whole system in the United States is that Churches aren't required to file a 990 no matter what their revenues and assets. This fuels the lack of transparency and accountability we need and enables the abuse we've seen so many times over the years. Church parsonages worth millions, jets and gold-plated toilets. Sheesh.

Another useful research tool is the ECFA or Evangelical Council for Financial Accountability. This is a voluntary body that ministries and churches can join and provide copies of their financial accounts each year. That information is public and searchable on the ECFA website to help bring confidence through transparency. It's not as useful as the 990 form, but it's fast and easy and a great place to start.

Now you might be thinking 'hey wait a minute Mike, you said we're supposed to take the lead and build something sustainable, using every resource you've got to bring it to life'.

I did. And I meant it.

But we aren't silos.

We were created for community. So if there's a way you can merge into an existing group and still achieve the goals we're laying out here, while fulfilling God's nudges in your heart, then do it. Every entrepreneur and business owner knows it's easier to take something and grow it, than build something from nothing.

Replicating something vs. improving something is a question only you can answer.

If that doesn't look like a possibility, then talk to them and tell them your dreams. Tell them what you're thinking and ask them for help. Ask them to show you the mistakes they made. Ask them to share with you the things they've learned. Ask them to support you in any way they can as you build out your mission objectives because remember, this isn't business.

We aren't competing.

We're all on the same team.

Team Jesus.

It's ok to work together because your success won't be at their expense.

The main goal here is for you to bring your team, your network, your influence and your capital to the forefront for Jesus and His mission. Partnering (not donating) with another organization *could* be one way to achieve this or at the very least, help you grow into a position where you're ready to lead the charge.

If you arrive at the conclusion you need to start something new, then creating a 501(c)3 is the first step. If you're still researching and trying to figure this all out but feeling an internal pressure to give then wait, don't make a rushed decision just to get the funds out of your hands by giving it to a church or organization that might not use it wisely, there's another option with tax advantages that can help until you're ready.

Investing in a 'Donor Managed Fund' is a simple, fast way to protect your capital, ensure it grows (they're typically ETF type accounts) while giving you the tax savings today, and the ability to give to projects tomorrow. It's a protected account so once you give, you can't ever pull back out from it for your own benefit, but it shows Jesus you're serious about earmarking capital for His mission, even when you haven't quite figured out what specific projects those funds should go to.

Another option is to connect with me online we're looking for others who resonate with this message, feel God's nudging and want to do more. Our hope is to connect like minded entrepreneurs, give you the ability to ask questions, receive coaching and more. If you're serious about investing in impact, let's talk.

I'll leave you with two final thoughts in all this.

1. Don't get busy just to make yourself feel better and feed the savior complex we all have inside of us.

It's there, it's real, and it's a problem.

Who doesn't feel good after helping someone else? Who

doesn't think that they're a better human being because they did something for another person? It's ok to feel that way, it's ok to think that way but only for a second.

No more.

Because we're not the saviors.

Jesus is.

We must be honest with ourselves and make sure that whatever we think God is nudging us to do, there's actually a problem to fix. Every great business succeeded because it fixed a problem in a way that was better than anyone else trying. This is no different and if we're not fixing a problem, we're just making ourselves busy. But there's enough busy-ness in the Church already, we don't need to add to it because being busy for Jesus won't deliver the results he's demanding from us.

2. It's ok to ask questions.

I don't know why but I've spoken to and seen too many successful, intelligent people throw out all reason and sound judgment when giving to Jesus.

For some reason we seem to think that we can build and grow businesses through our intellect and competencies, but when it comes to giving we're supposed to blindly write checks because someone else told us they're serving Jesus, and we believed them.

The good news is that if you've done that, it's not your fault. Your heart is soft and gentle towards your creator. It's a sign that God has created you to be a giver. To be an investor in the Kingdom of Jesus. It's a glimpse of your future and the journey so far has been a learning experience. It's why He's got you here reading this book.

But make no mistake, whether it was slick salesman talk or simply inexperience on your part, it's never ok to give large amounts of capital to anyone or anything without applying those same, critical thinking skills to it.

We might be led to give with our hearts, but we successfully give with our heads.

Ask questions.

Set milestones.

Have clear expectations as to what the funds will be used for.

Check and validate.

You'd never invest in a startup without checking into its founders, the financials of the company up to that point and so much more, so why give to a ministry or organization without doing the same. We'll answer for that one day because it's not being a good steward of what God has entrusted us with. We can't blame the other person for 'making us do it'. We can't blame our ignorance on just wanting to do something for Jesus. His expectation has been and always will be that we sow into areas with the biggest impact for Him. Our job is to find them, and then create them.

I give you permission today, to never again donate anything, anywhere, of any meaningful magnitude until you've researched and conducted the same amount of due diligence and care as you would any other business endeavor.

I don't think Jesus will hold it against you.

He'll thank you for it.

Just don't lose heart and give up, spending it on yourself.

I can't help you with that one!

Still got questions? That's ok too. This isn't a simple journey. It's something that's going to take the rest of your life to figure out and build. But if you'd like to be supported and maybe have a sherpa help you along the way get in touch and let's chat.

ACKNOWLEDGMENTS

I was going to start with something like the genealogy lists in the Bible but figured I wouldn't for two reasons. First, I'm not sure I need to thank my first grade teachers and second, no one reads them anyway.

In those timeless words spoken by Ricky Bobby, "if you ain't first, you're last", and so my amazing wife Linda has to be first. You read the same words over and over as I wrote, rewrote, and then rewrote the rewrites putting this masterpiece together.

You listened as I rambled, incessantly about some of the concepts within. You guided me as my directness needed to soften in a few places. But most of all you were just you, and the glow from your halo of amazingness warms my days. Every single one of them.

Troy, Chloe and Zak. You did a great job of being interested as you had to listen to so many of these themes being discussed between me and mom. My prayer is that you all find your way into God's best for your life, and recognize that entrepreneurship is exactly that.

Mom and Dad, thanks for all the encouragement on this book and for the many prayers that brought me here. It's time to move to Texas y'all.

And to my other parents, the American ones who adopted us into their family when they hired us as youth pastors over 20 years ago, Charles and Dianne. I literally wouldn't be here in Texas without you. By extension, the journey to this book might never have happened. Thanks for hearing God's voice. Many times over.

To Scott my publisher and coach. I never would have believed when we met, that we'd be singing 'Don't Stop Believin' together in Vegas just a few months later. Our early chats and your constant availability truly helped as the book began to take shape. Your editing team were a delight and far gentler on me than expected.

Leah, thanks for joining in on those occasions when I was fortunate enough to see you both. Your insights and encouragement went a long way to helping overcome some of the biggest obstacles. A.K.A. what to call the book!

Corban, Rosie, Andrew, Mom and rest of the gang who read the pre-release manuscript and provided thoughtful, helpful suggestions and edits. Ya'll rock and were just amazingly sweet in your feedback.

My incredible launch team, too many to name here. You all gave your time to help spread the word of this incredibly important message and we (hopefully) had a little fun along the way. Who knew that Zoom calls could actually be cool?!

Team WorkLodge, my crew who help live out the DNA and foundation of helping people. From those who came and went

(Vince, Jordan, Evan, Tim and others) to my present day team led by Michelle. You've done an amazing job of helping create the time for me to put this work together while being flexible as I've worked on a launch plan that moved more than a few times.

Thanks to all the guests who've joined me on The Mike Thakur Show (Jordan Raynor, Perry Marshall, Daniel Fusco, Taylor Hughes, Kim Stuart, Britt Mooney and so many more). The conversations we've had, the thoughts you shared and the wisdom I was able to glean from helped me as I shaped these thoughts and threw a few selfish questions your way.

And finally Bob Goff. Thank you so much for being kind enough to lend your support and a few words to this project. Getting to know you and seeing another entrepreneur in love with Jesus has been such an encouragement, I can't wait to party with you in Uganda as we look over your project, there.

Is it cheesy to thank Jesus or will it get get eye rolls like those actors at the Oscars because everyone just assumed those thanks go without saying? Either way, you're amazing and it's always been all about you. I'm just grateful you were an entrepreneur too. If I had to imitate walking on water, I'd be cold and wet. Two things that go together like chalk and cheese.

ABOUT THE AUTHOR

Mike Thakur is one of Houston's 'Most Admired CEOs' and host of 'The Mike Thakur Show' podcast.

Beginning his entrepreneurial journey in the UK as co-founder of an internet consultancy, he flip-flopped his time between senior roles for a billion-dollar IT solutions provider with breaks to pursue ministry and mission related roles.

In 2007 Mike moved his family to the US. He spent several years in the nonprofit world before joining The Guidry Group, a boutique private security firm affectionately nicknamed the 'Secret Service for Billionaires'. They specialized in kidnap, ransom and extortion cases, and during his time there, Mike assumed the role of Chief Operating Officer.

He believes that entrepreneurship, fused with faith is the fundamental vehicle for bringing sustainable change to society's biggest humanitarian issues both at home and abroad. With a lifetime of work in ministry and a deep passion for both business and service, he created a co-working company, Work-Lodge as a social enterprise on a mission to change lives along with FT5K (Feed the Five Thousand), a 501(c)3 solely funded by WorkLodge to bring hope to the hopeless, through self-sustaining one off projects.

When he's not inspiring his team and clients to 'Be Amazing,' you'll find him communicating his message on YouTube and everywhere Podcasts play.

Mike is involved with several faith-based 501(c)(3) organizations committed to helping those who can't help themselves and currently resides in Houston, Texas with his wife, Linda, and three children, Troy, Chloe and Zak.

CONNECT WITH MIKE

www.mikethakur.com/beamazing

CPSIA information can be obtained
at www.ICGtesting.com
Printed in the USA
JSHW030406130322
23711JS00001B/5